About the Authors

Brian Nolan is a Research Professor and Dr Dorothy Watson is a
Research Officer at The Economic and Social Research Institute.

WOMEN AND POVERTY
IN IRELAND

Brian Nolan
Dorothy Watson

Oak Tree Press
Dublin
in association with
Combat Poverty Agency

Oak Tree Press
Merrion Building
Lower Merrion Street
Dublin 2, Ireland
www.oaktreepress.com

© 1999 Combat Poverty Agency

A catalogue record of this book is
available from the British Library.

ISBN 1 86076 136 4

This study forms part of the Combat Poverty Agency's Research
Series, in which it is No. 27. The views expressed in this report are
the authors' own and not necessarily those of the
Combat Poverty Agency.

Printed in the Republic of Ireland
by Colour Books Ltd.

CONTENTS

LIST OF TABLES

ACKNOWLEDGEMENTS

This study draws extensively on data obtained in the 1994 Living in Ireland Survey. Brendan Whelan and James Williams of the ESRI's Survey Unit were responsible for the survey design, data collection and database creation. The authors received valuable comments on earlier drafts from the Combat Poverty Agency and the Department of Social, Community and Family Affairs, and from participants at a workshop organised by the Agency. The authors have benefited greatly from discussions on various aspects of the study with ESRI colleagues Tim Callan, Chris Whelan and James Williams, collaborators in the broader programme of research based on the Living in Ireland Surveys within which this study fits. The authors are particularly grateful to Chris Whelan for his permission to report some early results from his work on psychological distress. The authors have also drawn on joint work with Sara Cantillon, Centre for Equality Studies, UCD on intra-household inequalities.

The Combat Poverty Agency would like to thank Brian Nolan and Dorothy Watson for their work on this study and all of those who commented on earlier drafts and whose insights contributed to shaping the final report. Recognising the wide range of expertise on women's issues in Ireland, the Agency organised a workshop on this study in May, 1998, to which relevant organisations were invited. This provided an invaluable opportunity to discuss methodological issues and findings and thanks is extended to participants.

Finally, the Agency also acknowledges the work of Helen Johnston and Carmel Corrigan of its Research Section in managing this project and Joan O'Flynn and Clare Farrell for editorial and production work on the publication.

FOREWORD

Introduction

The aim of the Combat Poverty Agency is to work for the prevention and elimination of poverty and social exclusion in Ireland. In pursuing this aim, the Agency is particularly interested in highlighting the position and circumstances of groups most at risk of poverty and inequality. In addition, the Agency is concerned with exploring and promoting a greater understanding of the causes of poverty, exclusion and inequality and the often complex interaction of factors that contribute to the position of individuals and groups with respect to poverty.

In its work, the relative position of women in Ireland, their access to resources, including adequate income, economic and employment opportunities, and their experience of poverty has been an ongoing concern of the Agency and has been the focus of a number of reports[1] and pilot initiatives. The current study arose from findings presented in *Poverty in the 1990s* (Callan *et al.*).[2] Contrary to the trend found between 1973 and 1987, that report clearly pointed to a substantial increase in the risk of poverty experienced by households headed by women between 1987 and 1994. Given the detailed information now available through the

---

[1] See Daly, M. (1989) *Women and Poverty* (with Attic Press); Combat Poverty Agency (1990) *Towards a Policy for Combating Poverty Among Women*; O'Neill, C. (1992) *Telling it Like It Is*.

[2] Callan, T., Nolan, B., Whelan, B., Whelan, C. and Williams, J. (1996), *Poverty in the 1990s; Evidence from the Living in Ireland Survey*. Dublin: Oak Tree Press in association with the Combat Poverty Agency, ESRI, Dept. of Social, Community and Family Affairs.

Living in Ireland Survey, the Agency commissioned this study to explore in greater depth the factors contributing to this increasing risk.

Background

This study was undertaken by Professor Brian Nolan and Dr Dorothy Watson of The Economic and Social Research Institute (ESRI). It is based on data from the ESRI 1987 survey of household income, and the results of the 1994 Living in Ireland Survey, the most recent year for which complete data is available. The study focuses on three core issues: the increasing risk of poverty among female-headed households; the interaction of low pay and household poverty; and the incidence of "hidden" deprivation experienced by women within households. This focus was determined by a number of factors. Principal among these was the policy function and concern of the Agency, previous research and the nature and scope of the information available from the Living in Ireland Survey.

The approach adopted by the authors allows for the comparison of women in varying household situations. In addition to examining women's risk of poverty compared to that of men, the study presents an analysis based on comparisons between female- male- and couple-headed households. Comparisons between women who are household heads and those who occupy other positions within households are also presented, as is an analysis of individual access to non-monetary resources within couple headed households. This approach highlights the factors affecting the risk of poverty for women and clearly recognises that women's experience of poverty is not a homogeneous one.

Increasing Poverty Among Female-Headed Households

This report takes as its starting point the substantial increase in the risk of poverty among female-headed households between 1987 and 1994. The risk of poverty for women who live alone and for lone mother households at the 50 per cent relative poverty line rose particularly sharply during this period from four to 24 per cent and 17 to 32 per cent respectively. By 1994, their risk of poverty was substantially higher than that of households headed by couples, by men living alone or male lone parents, whose poverty risk decreased slightly or remained unchanged. Changes in the profile of female-headed households, in their composition and the economic status of the adults account for about one third of the increased risk.

The authors conclude that the most important factor contributing to the increase in poverty risk for female-headed households is the level of welfare payments on which many lone parent and households headed by single women rely. In the period from 1987 to 1994, welfare policy concentrated on increasing the lowest social welfare payments as part of a long-term strategy to bring them into line with the adequate minimum rate recommended by the Commission on Social Welfare.[3] For households headed by women dependent on these payments, these increases reduced their depth of poverty by bringing them closer to the poverty line but were insufficient to lift them out of poverty.

Over the same period, other social welfare payments, including old age pensions, increased more slowly. As a result, by 1994 households headed by older people dependent on such pensions fell further below the poverty line and this has resulted in the observed increased poverty risk for households headed by older women. It is important to acknowledge that old age pensions have increased substantially since 1994 and that a political commitment to increase them further to £100 per week by 2002 is in place. In addition, many elderly households are in receipt of a range of non-cash benefits, such as free telephone rental, free electricity allowance and free travel, which are not available to other welfare recipients. Their impact on the position of older women living alone is not taken into account in the current study.

From a policy perspective, the issue of adequate income support for lone parent households, the vast majority of which are headed by women, emerges as a clear priority. A number of options are evident here, the two most obvious being increasing the level of welfare payments to lone parents in line with increases in average earnings and removing barriers to participation in the labour market. In this regard the role of child benefit

---

[3] Government of Ireland (1986), *Report of the Commission on Social Welfare*. Dublin: The Stationery Office.

as an anti-poverty measure is important and the Agency has consistently argued for substantial increases to this payment. In clearly identifying families with dependent children as among those with the highest risk of poverty, and the particularly vulnerable position of lone mother households, the study lends support to this argument.

The Impact of Living Arrangements

The authors state clearly that it is the growing number of women living alone and female lone parent households that is driving the increase in the risk of poverty experienced by women. At the level of the individual, women also face a higher risk than men of living in a poor household. However, the difference in the risk of poverty between men and women at the individual level is much less than that between female-headed households and male and couple headed households. This is primarily because most adult women live in couple households, which in general face a lower risk of poverty. This difference in individual and household poverty risks leads to the question of the extent to which occupying a status other than household head insulates women from poverty. The authors concentrate their attention on unattached women and female lone parents (under 45 years of age) living in households in which they are not household head. One of the key findings to emerge is that the degree of protection from poverty provided by living in a household in which they were not the household head is closely related to economic status. If not in paid employment, living in households in which they were not the household head substantially reduces the risk of poverty for young unattached men, women and lone mothers.

These findings, however, must be interpreted with care and their long-term implications carefully considered. They do not take account of the incidence or impact of overcrowding, or of the impact of delayed independent living on both young individuals and their families. It is important to recognise that the lesson emerging here is not one of promoting that all single adults and many lone mothers remain in or return to their family home well into adulthood, but that the establishment of independent households should not result in increased poverty. The current housing market, rapidly increasing house prices and private rents, coupled with an inadequate supply of local authority housing has made the establishment of independent households an unobtainable aspiration for many young adults and lone parents, particularly those on low incomes. If independent living is to be encouraged and overcrowding avoided, new and innovative ways of providing opportunities for the establishment of independent households that do not result in poverty must be explored.

The Role of Women's Pay

In examining the role of women's earnings in combating poverty, the study restates the position of women in relation to low pay and part-time work. Women are more likely to be part-time workers, part-time work is more often low paid, therefore women are more likely to be low paid. However, it is important to note that even in full-time employment, women are more likely to be low paid than their male counterparts.

The distinction made in the study between the economic status of the household head and that of other members living in the household is an important one as it highlights the role of earnings, irrespective of whose they are, in raising households above the poverty line. The study points out that there is in fact a limited relationship between low pay and household poverty, with few households in which there is at least one person employed falling below the poverty line. However, of the minority of employees who live in poor households, it is noteworthy that over half of these are in low paid jobs. Focusing on women employees in poor households, these are more likely to be low paid and in part-time employment. The authors are also clear that women's pay, even low pay, can have a significant role in keeping households out of poverty, and estimate that approximately one quarter of households containing a low paid woman would fall below the poverty line were her earnings not available.

These findings raise a number of issues of concern to the Agency in relation to women's labour market participation. The first relates to low pay. The proposed introduction of the national minimum wage has the potential to benefit low paid workers, the majority of whom are women. However, it is unclear as yet how the minimum wage will operate and what its implications will be for workers in varying circumstances. This is an area that will require close monitoring to ensure that poverty traps do not arise as a result of the operation of the minimum wage and its interaction with the tax and social welfare systems.

The second set of issues relates to women's access to paid employment. It is very clear from the findings presented in the report that paid employment is the most efficient route out of poverty for women, and particularly for those heading households in their own right. In the current economic boom, where there is growing evidence of a shortage of both skilled and unskilled workers to meet the market demand, removing barriers to women's labour market participation has advantages for both women and the economy and society generally. In this context it is essential that access to training, education and employment opportunities be provided for those women who wish to take them up. This needs to be supported by the provision of adequate, affordable and appropriate childcare and the broad adoption of family-friendly policies. It is essential, however, that such provision is provided in the context of an integrated tax and social welfare system that does not contain or generate poverty and unemployment traps. With regard to childcare, the study acknowledges that universal support to families through child benefit is the best option from an anti-poverty perspective. The Agency strongly supports this view, but stresses that it is important that this form part of an anti-poverty strategy to support all families, rather than being restricted to those engaged in labour market activities.

"Hidden" Intra-Household Poverty

The majority of the analysis presented in this study is based on the assumption that resources in households are shared equally between its members. This assumption is broadly held in surveys of household income. However, it has been frequently argued that women's poverty may arise through the uneven distribution of resources within households and is thereby "hidden" in household analyses.

Drawing on the 1987 ESRI Survey of Household Income, the study presents a summary analysis of levels of non-monetary lifestyle deprivation expressed by husbands and wives. Spouses were asked if they lacked a number of items, including an annual holiday, a hobby or leisure activity and a warm overcoat, due to lack of money. Using this scale, it was found that women reported only slightly higher deprivation scores than their husbands and that the majority of couples in fact reported an agreed level of deprivation. The authors argue that it is a range of factors related to the household, including the economic status and unemployment experience of the household head, that are the best predictors of individual levels of deprivation among household members. In relation to women's experience of poverty, the authors conclude that the evidence does not appear to support the notion that conventional poverty measures miss substantial numbers of poor women in non-poor households. However, the authors point out that the indicators used were not specifically designed to capture gender differences in access to household resources or to measure the extent to which there are inequities in the distribution of resources within households. This analysis reveals nothing, nor can it be expected to, of the balance of power relationships within households in relation to the control and allocation of income and other resources. This is an area that requires more in-depth research utilising more sensitive measurements.

The Changing Policy Context

Since the 1994 Living in Ireland Survey, a number of policy initiatives have taken place. Although the majority do not specifically aim to address the issue, if implemented many of their recommendations will have an influence on women and their experience of poverty. Of particular note among these are the Report of the Expert Working Group on Integration of the Tax and Social Welfare System (1996)[4], the Report of the Commission on the Family (1998)[5], the Review of Community Employment (1998)[6] and the forthcoming reports of the Tax and Welfare Treatment of

---

[4] Integrating Tax and Social Welfare — Report of the Expert Working Group on the Integration of the Tax and Social Welfare Systems (1996), Dublin: Stationery Office.

[5] Commission on the Family (1998), Strengthening Families for Life, Final Report to the Minister for Social, Community and Family Affairs, Dublin: Stationery Office.

[6] Murphy, T., Deloitte and Touche (1998), Review of Community Employment Programme Final Report, Dublin: The Stationery Office.

Households Group and the Expert Working Group on Childcare. This study adds to the knowledge of women's poverty available to those deliberating either on the implementation of these initiatives or their forthcoming recommendations.

It also has a particular relevance in the context of the National Anti-Poverty Strategy (NAPS). One of the seven principles underlying this strategy is "the reduction of inequalities and in particular, addressing the gender dimensions of poverty".[7] In addition, the NAPS identified households headed by a single adult, those headed by someone engaged in home duties and lone parents as being among those particularly at risk of poverty. There is considerable overlap between these groups and women.

The study bears out that women experience a greater risk of poverty than men, female-headed households a greater risk than those headed by men or couples and identifies groups of women who are particularly vulnerable to poverty. Through NAPS, the introduction of poverty-proofing by government departments of all substantial policy proposals and the equality-proofing of these by the National Economic and Social Forum provides additional mechanisms whereby the interests of those at risk of poverty, including groups of women, can be both promoted and protected. This study also clearly indicates that single policy responses are unlikely to improve the situation for women. Instead what will be required are integrated responses that reflect the complexities of women's lives. Increased inter-departmental co-operation being fostered by the NAPS and through the Strategic Management Initiative in the public service should contribute to the achievement of such approaches. If successful, these initiatives will provide some of the means necessary to combat poverty among women.

Concluding Remarks

In commissioning this study the Agency was aware that no one study could address the wide and complex range of issues that fall into the broad arena of gender inequalities. While the data on which this study is based can provide a broad overview of women's

---

[7] Sharing in Progress: National Anti-Poverty Strategy (1997), Dublin: The Stationery Office.

risk of poverty, it cannot provide the in-depth insights required to examine all aspects of gender inequalities. As with all household studies it also captures only those who reside in private households. Therefore some of the most vulnerable groups of women — those in refuges or hostels, Travellers, refugees, women in institutional care and homeless women — are not included here.

Qualitative research studies and local case studies inform us that it is women who bear the brunt of poverty. While reflecting structural inequalities, their experiences of poverty and inequalities are frequently both very personal and sensitive, particularly for those women in the most vulnerable situations. Their perspective, however, is critical to understanding the gender dimension of poverty. To explore these issues the development of qualitative research tools and methods that capture women's experiences of poverty and inequality, elucidate their coping mechanisms and identify their needs are required. With regard to the current Living in Ireland Survey, this and other household surveys could be further used to investigate men and women's different experiences of poverty through the inclusion of questions or modules specifically designed to capture such information. This approach should not only apply to gender inequalities but also to other inequalities prevalent in society such as those based on race.

Combat Poverty Agency
April 1999

GLOSSARY

Coefficients: In statistical equations, a coefficient is a number which describes the effect of each explanatory variable on the dependent variable.

Iterative procedures: In developing the explanatory models in Chapters 3 and 4, we used an iterative procedure to decide which variables to drop and which to keep. This was not a formal statistical iteration, of the kind that might be used, for instance, in maximum likelihood estimation. Instead, it involved a careful examination of changes in the coefficients in a model as variables are added and removed in order to gain an understanding of the interplay of the different effects on poverty risk.

Logarithmic form: Variables such as income are often analysed in logarithmic form. This means examining the effects of the natural log of income rather than the actual amount of income. Using the log of income has the effect of giving greater "weight" to a given (for instance, £10) change in income at lower income levels than at higher income levels.

Logit models: A logit regression model is used to examine the effects of different factors (such as age, household type) on a dependent variable (poverty in this case) which has a number of categories (poor and not poor) rather than being measured on a continuum (such as income). The coefficients in the models show the impact of each explanatory variable on the (log of the) odds of being under the 50 per cent poverty line. Since the coefficients do not have an intuitive interpretation, the results are also presented in terms of the poverty rate we would expect for certain groups which vary in terms of the factors we are interested in.

Multicollinearity: This refers to a situation in statistical models where two or more explanatory variables are so closely associated in the data that it is not possible to separate their effects on the dependent variable we are interested in.

Regression: This refers to a range of statistical techniques which can be used to examine the effect of an explanatory variable (or a set of explanatory variables) on a dependent variable. For instance, we might use regression analysis to look at the effects on poverty risk or household income (the dependent variables) of explanatory variables such as household size, household type, number of members at work, and so on.

Statistically Significant: This is a term which is used when we can be confident (typically at the 95 per cent 'confidence level') that an effect which is found in the sample reflects a real effect in the population we are studying, rather than being due to sampling error.

Chapter 1

INTRODUCTION

Introduction

This study is concerned with women and poverty in Ireland. The National Anti-Poverty Strategy adopted by the government in 1997 has, as part of its guiding principles, "the reduction of inequalities and in particular addressing the gender dimension of poverty" (p. 7). There are many topics within the broad compass of women and poverty that it would be extremely valuable to explore, but a single study cannot hope to deal satisfactorily with them all, much less the broader gender inequalities within which they must be seen. Rather than attempting to provide an overview across the diverse range of topics that could come under the heading of women and poverty, then, we seek to investigate a number of specific issues in some depth.

The study concentrates on three core elements. These are:

- How and why the risk of poverty for households headed by women versus those headed by couples or men, and the risk of poverty for women versus men, have been changing;

- The extent and nature of low pay for women in employment and how it relates to household poverty; and,

- What non-monetary indicators of deprivation can tell us about the distribution of resources and the extent of "hidden poverty" among women within the household.

These distinct elements arise out of previous research, and are of direct relevance to the formulation of anti-poverty policy. They have also featured extensively in both national and international debates and discussions on the causes and implications of poverty for women. The aim of the study is to enhance understanding of these issues, contribute to current policy formulation, and point towards ways in which research on them might profitably proceed in the future. By building on what has been learned about women and poverty from previous research at the ESRI and elsewhere, the study is intended to contribute in particular to the on-going evolution of an effective anti-poverty strategy in Ireland.

Recent Research on Women and Poverty

The feminisation of poverty, the male–female wage gap particularly as it relates to low pay, and what we might broadly term intra-household inequalities between men and women have been central themes of recent research and debate on women and poverty in the industrialised countries. Rather than comprehensively reviewing this extensive literature, here we simply aim to sketch out key features with a bearing on the current study, and then briefly discuss recent studies relevant to Ireland.

The Feminisation of Poverty

The feminisation of poverty is a term and theme emanating originally from the USA and strongly influenced by US experience. It was first used by Diana Pearce (1978) to describe the increase between the late 1960s and late 1970s in the proportion of poor households in the United States that were headed by women. During that period the poverty rate of mother-only families changed very little but that of two-parent families declined, while the proportion of persons living in mother-only households increased. It was these two factors, rather than an increased risk of poverty for mother-only families *per se*, that produced the observed "feminisation of poverty" in the United States (Garfinkel and McLanahan, 1986; Northrop, 1990).

As well as the declining fortunes of female-headed households, the term feminisation of poverty has also been used more broadly to refer to an increasing proportion of poor adults who are female, also a feature of recent US experience (McLanahan, Sørensen and Watson, 1989). It is however important to maintain the distinction between these two phenomena, since the relationships between them can be complex.

The "feminisation of poverty" theme has seen a great deal of research in the USA, by economists and sociologists. This has concentrated on factors leading to the rise in the proportion of "female-headed" households (particularly marital breakdown, non-marital births and widowhood), and on the changing composition of female-headed households (in terms of race, marital status and age of the female head). Debates have also centered on whether the "feminisation of poverty" is a uniquely American phenomenon (Abowitz, 1986; Goldberg *et al*, 1990; Marklund, 1990; Norris, 1984) and on the extent to which it applies equally to different races or different age groups within a country (Bose, 1989; Arber and Ginn, 1991; Hardy and Hazelrigg, 1993). Goldberg and Kremen (1987), in a review of the position of female-headed households in seven countries concluded that the feminisation of poverty is not uniquely American, but is most pronounced in the United States. Goldberg *et al* (1990) point to the importance of labour market and family policies in countries such as France and Sweden in preventing poverty from becoming feminised in these countries. Wright (1992) examines UK evidence and concludes that the feminisation of poverty did not occur there. Marklund (1990) argues that the feminisation of poverty, (like marginalisation of the poor or underclass ideas) is not relevant to the recent experience of the Scandinavian countries. Outside the USA, lone parenthood *per se* has tended to receive attention beyond the implications it might have for the feminisation of poverty (see, for example, Ermisch, Jenkins and Wright, 1989).

While the notion of feminisation of poverty has served as a very useful spur to research, questions have also been raised regarding the utility of the concept, particularly in terms of the gender-biased notion that in households containing a couple the man is taken as head. "Female-headed households" are thus those where the "head" is a single, divorced, or widowed woman rather than a man or couple. The implicit assumption of equal distribution of resources within households underlying the use of household-based analysis has also been questioned, as we discuss below. Other critics of the focus on the feminisation of poverty have been concerned that it leads to a tendency to overlook broader issues.

Sheak (1988), for example, argues that it can obscure the larger economic and political roots of poverty, since the feminisation of poverty tended to be less pronounced in periods when the poverty rate was rising. Income poverty may also not tell the whole story, of course: Sakamoto (1988) argues that if well-being is considered in terms of poverty and mortality jointly, there has been no decline in women's well-being relative to men between 1960 and 1980 in the US.

Women and Low Pay

The overall gap between male and female wages has been a focus of research internationally for many years and has spawned research on a wide range of sub-themes. These include differences between men and women in the financial returns they receive for educational attainment and work experience (Duncan, 1996; Felstead, 1996; Terrell, 1992), segmented labour markets (Blau, 1993; Boston, 1990; Marini and Fan, 1997; Petersen and Morgan, 1995; Skvoretz and Smith, 1990; Taris, 1996), the impact of collective bargaining (Rosenfeld and Kalleberg, 1991), male–female differences in work-related preferences (Ross and Mirowsky, 1996; Rowe and Snizek, 1995), career interruption, part-time workers and overtime (Brereton, 1990). Policy debates have also led to research concentrated on legislation on comparable worth, equal opportunities, and reverse discrimination, as well as the working poor and minimum wage legislation (Baron and Newman, 1990; Blackburn, 1995; Figart and Lapidus, 1995; Rubery, 1993). Recent research in the United States has pointed to a shrinking of the wage gap, although the reasons have as much to do with increasing inequality in the earnings of white men as improvements in women's earnings (Bernhardt, Morris and Handcock, 1995).

From a poverty perspective, however, it is the concentration of women in low-paid employment rather than the male–female wage gap along the entire spectrum of pay rates that is of primary importance. What Harkness *et al* call the "pin-money" hypothesis holds that the over-representation of women amongst the low-paid is of little importance for poverty because women's earnings account for only a small proportion of family income. However, they find that women's earnings in Britain are playing an increasingly important role in keeping families out of poverty (Harkness, Machin and Waldfogel, 1997). Rubery (1993) argues that the current wage structure reflects an outdated model of social and family organisation, and that much poverty is now the result of women seeking economic independence in a market which regards them as subordinate family members.

Intra-Household Inequality and Poverty

Most research on poverty relies on income as the measure of living standards or poverty status, and adopts the household as the income sharing unit. (A household is conventionally defined as a single person or group of people regularly living in the same accommodation and sharing catering arrangements — not necessarily relatives.) This means that either a household's income is below an income poverty line and everyone in that household will be counted as poor, or income is not below the poverty line and none of them will be counted as poor. While reliance on the household (and on income) has many advantages, it may mask significant inequalities between household members, and the implications these may have for poverty among women. Studies by Davies and Joshi (1994) and by Findlay and Wright (1996), for example, illustrate that the assumptions made regarding the sharing of income within households could have a crucial impact on measurement of the incidence of poverty. A major challenge in dealing with issues of intra-household distribution of resources, however, is in the difficulty involved in measuring inequalities in this respect.

It is also important to consider not only inequalities within existing households but also what would happen to the household members as individuals if they were to disperse. The fact that women's access to the economic resources of the household is contingent on remaining in the relationship with the main breadwinner has particular implications in the event of marital breakdown. Research in other countries has shown that women and children fare worse than men economically in the event of divorce (Arditti, 1997; Finnie, 1993). Other lines of research in this area indicate that women's access to pension benefits is also affected detrimentally by divorce, and by the reduced number of years spent in paid work because of childcare and household responsibilities (Ginn and Arber, 1991; Hatch, 1990; Meyer, 1990).

Research on access to non-economic resources centers on whether the responsibility for children and for housework is unequally distributed between men and women (Doucet, 1995). Because of differences in time spent caring for children and on housework, women's labour force participation is limited in terms of the distance they can travel to work, the need to find scarce childcare or interrupt their careers, and their freedom to travel as part of the job (Howell and Bronson, 1996; Semyonov and Epstein, 1991; Presser and Hermsen, 1996). The unequal distribution of responsibility for unpaid housework also reduces women's access to leisure time (Green and Woodward, 1990), with the gender gap being more marked in "high family workload" situations (Shaw, 1991). Intra-household inequalities, then, may take the form of unequal access at a given point in time to the economic resources of a household (so that, for instance, more resources are available to men than to women and children); unequal contingent access to these resources (so that leaving the marriage would mean a greater loss of resources to one partner than to the other); or unequal access to non-economic resources such as leisure time.

Psychological research has suggested that men and women view and accept responsibility differently. Heimer (1996), for instance, suggests that while men accept responsibilities as strategic opportunities or investments, women view responsibilities as fates that limit their capacities to strategise and invest outside the family, which often means putting the needs of others ahead of one's own.

Irish Research on Women and Poverty

Research on poverty in Ireland in the 1970s and into the 1980s presented a picture of the overall extent of poverty and the types of household most at risk, relying on data from administrative statistics and the Household Budget Surveys of 1973 and 1980 (Ó Cinnéide, 1972; Kennedy 1981; Roche, 1984; Joyce and McCashin, 1982; Rottman, Hannan, Hardiman and Wiley 1982. For a review see Callan, Nolan *et al* (1989), Chapter 3). Most of the emphasis in these studies was on the variation in poverty risk and composition of the poor by labour force status of the household head, urban/rural location, age and lifecycle stage, and household composition.[1] Particular groups which emerged as facing a relatively high risk included some households headed by women (rather than a couple or man), notably widows in the early 1970s, and the overall risk for men versus women was on occasion presented — for example, by Roche (1984). However, feminisation of poverty had not emerged as a concern at that point, nor was the possible implication for women's poverty of intra-household inequalities an important theme in this research.

The first results published from the analysis of poverty using the 1987 ESRI household survey, in Callan, Nolan *et al* (1989), included an analysis of trends over time in the risk facing female-headed versus male-headed households (with the latter including couple-headed households). This showed the risk of being below income poverty lines declining sharply for female-headed households between 1973 and 1987. As a result, by 1987 female-headed households faced a below-average risk of falling below half mean income and a marginally above-average risk of falling below 60 per cent of that mean, whereas at the start of the period they had a very much higher risk than other households at both these lines. This was seen to reflect the substantial improvement over the period in the relative position of the elderly (see Callan, Nolan *et al*, (1989), Table 7.6, p. 100). Analysis at the level of the narrower tax unit rather than household showed female-headed tax units at about or below the average poverty risk.

Around the same time, Daly (1989) reviewed available evidence on various aspects of women and poverty in Ireland, including women's experience of poverty; the relationship between women's work and poverty, the social welfare system and women, women's access to education; housing and the law; and, poverty and women's health. Daly placed particular emphasis on the argument that women and perhaps children are likely to be undercounted in poverty figures that are based on household or family income. She sought to identify particular groups of women likely to be most at risk of poverty, notably women rearing children on their own; elderly women; Travellers and homeless women; women in low-

---

[1] Kennedy (1981), for example, had separate chapters on urban poverty, rural poverty, poverty and old people, and poverty and homelessness but not on women and poverty.

paying jobs; and some women working full-time in the home. The information employed to support conclusions about the poverty rates facing some of these groups and the shortcomings of the conventional usage of the household as income recipient unit was, however, extremely patchy.[2] In discussing the particular nature of women's experience of poverty and survival strategies, the role of control and management of resources within the household was emphasised drawing on British evidence.

Low pay in general, but affecting many women, had been the subject of studies by Blackwell (1986) and McMahon (1987) drawing on data from around 1980, with Blackwell (1987) focusing specifically on low pay and women. The 1987 ESRI survey provided the basis for Nolan's (1993) analysis of the extent and composition of low pay at that date, which brought out once again the much higher probability of low pay for women than men employees and the concentration of low-paid women in certain sectors. It also quantified the extent to which, even after controlling for age, marital status, education, occupational group and industrial sector, women faced a higher probability than men of being low paid (see Callan, Nolan *et al*, 1989, Table 7.6, p. 100).

Further research based on the 1987 ESRI survey covered a variety of other areas relating to women and poverty, as summarised in Callan's chapter on "Poverty and Gender Inequality" in the overview volume edited by Nolan and Callan (1994). This reviewed the results of studies dealing with the risk of poverty for women versus men and for female-headed versus other households and tax units, labour market participation by women and the factors affecting it, and male–female wage differentials. These results are described in more detail in Callan and Farrell (1991) and Callan and Wren (1994), and we will not attempt to summarise them again here. In the same volume, Whelan (1994) (drawing on the more detailed Whelan, Hannan and Creighton, 1991) looked at the impact of unemployment and poverty on levels of psychological distress, including the impact on wives of their husbands' unemployment. This showed for example that husbands' unemployment resulted in heightened levels of psychological dis-

---

[2] The same is true of Duffy's (1994) discussion of poverty among a similar set of groups of women.

tress for wives when it resulted in the household being in poverty, but not otherwise.

Rottman's (1994) chapter "Allocating Money Within House-holds: Better Off Poorer?" in the same volume summarises the results of his in-depth study for the Combat Poverty Agency of the way resources are distributed within households (Rottman, 1993). This used results from a follow-up to the 1987 ESRI survey carried out in 1989, which contained questions on the way family finances were managed. This allowed households to be classified into different management/allocation systems — for example, where one person is responsible for all routine purchases from a "kitty", or there is shared management or independent management by the two spouses. An exploratory analysis was also carried out of the consequences that alternative allocation systems had for the standard of living enjoyed by different family members, based on a very limited set of measures such as access to personal spending money. The conclusions reached were that the consequences of how household finances are managed are quite significant for the well-being of individual members, but that — tentatively — the results did not lend credence to the notion that substantial numbers of women and children live in "hidden poverty" in non-poor households. Analysis by Cantillon (1994, 1997) and Cantillon and Nolan (1998) on this topic using non-monetary indicators from the 1987 ESRI survey, which came to similar conclusions, is discussed in detail in Chapter 6 below.

A vivid picture of, among other things, the way women manage resources in low income families in a particular Dublin community is given in O'Neill's (1992) study, also for the Combat Poverty Agency. This aims to convey a picture of different aspects of how poverty is experienced in that community, largely in the words of women living there. A number of detailed case studies are also presented, bringing out, *inter alia*, the strain on women coping with family poverty and the effect this has on their physical and psychological health. (The earlier Combat Poverty publication by Hayes (1990) describing and evaluating three women's projects also provides valuable contextual information on women's experience of poverty).[3]

Lone parents, a particularly high poverty risk group among women, have also been the subject of a number of recent studies.[4] Millar, Davies and Leaper (1992) and McCashin (1993) provided analysis of the extent and nature of lone parenthood and how this evolved over time, together with a discussion of options for policy. McCashin (1996) presents the results of a qualitative in-depth study of a small number of lone parents in one area of Dublin, including their routes into lone parenthood, support networks, financial circumstances and aspirations for the future. High income poverty rates and rates of deprivation were indeed found for these lone mothers. The findings emphasised the positive aspirations of many of the lone mothers to work or return to work when their children were older, the importance of childcare in making that possible, and the central role child benefit plays as a stable and direct payment to mothers (whether lone parents or not). McCashin (1997) provides an updated analysis of demographic and socio-economic trends in relation to lone parenthood, highlighting data and measurement problems, and examines participation in the labour market by lone parents and how that might be advanced.

We will not attempt to deal here with the range of other recent studies which, while clearly of relevance, are not directly focused on women and poverty. These include research on gender differences in education (e.g. Kelleghan and Fontes, 1988; Lynch, 1989; Hannan *et al*, 1996), women's health (e.g. Wiley and Merriman, 1996), the costs of children (e.g. Conniffe and Keogh, 1988; Carney *et al*, 1994), women's employment and unemployment (e.g. Blackwell, 1989; Walsh, 1993; Durkan, 1995; Sexton and O'Connell, 1997; Smyth, 1997), marital breakdown (including Ward, 1991; and Fahey and Lyons, 1995), and the various discussions of tax

---

[3] Drawing on such qualitative studies and the published results from the ESRI survey, Graham (1994) presented a review of the evidence then available on trends in family poverty and the experience of mothers coping on a low income in Ireland.

[4] See also Richardson and Winston's (1989) study based on a sample of non-marital births in one of Dublin's maternity hospitals.

and social welfare reforms which would *inter alia* affect women (for example, Callan and Nolan, 1994; McCashin, 1997; Clarke and Healy, 1997; Callan, O'Donoghue and O'Neill, 1994).

The final piece of research to be discussed here, and a key point of departure for the present study, is Callan *et al*'s (1996) presentation of first results from the 1994 Living in Ireland Survey carried out by the ESRI. As discussed in more detail in Chapter 2, this showed, among other things, an increase between 1987 and 1994 in the risk of income poverty facing single adult households, the elderly, and households headed by someone working full-time in the home — with a good deal of overlap between these groups. A related finding was a sharp increase in the risk of poverty facing households headed by a woman, whereas the risk for those headed by a man or a couple was rather stable over the period (see Callan *et al*, 1996, Table 5.6, p. 94). This represented a reversal of the downward trend in poverty risk of female-headed households which took place between 1973 and 1987, and explaining why it occurred is an important element in the present study.

The Data

The data to be employed in this study come from two large-scale household surveys carried out by the ESRI. The first is the Survey of Income Distribution, Poverty and Usage of State Services carried out in 1987, which obtained responses from a sample of 3,294 households, with a response rate of 64 per cent of valid addresses contacted. The sampling frame was the Register of Electors and the survey was designed to provide a national sample from the population resident in private households. The sample has been reweighted to correct for non-response, on the basis of four variables — number of adults in the household, urban/rural location, age and socio-economic group of household head — using external information from the much larger Labour Force Survey. The representativeness of this sample data has been validated by comparison with a variety of external information, and it has been used extensively in research on poverty and tax and social welfare policy in Ireland. A full description of the survey is in Callan, Nolan *et al.* (1989), and an overview of that research is in Nolan and Callan (1994).

The more recent source of data is the 1994 Living in Ireland Survey, the first wave of the Irish element of the European Community Household Panel (ECHP) being carried out for Eurostat by the ESRI. This obtained information from 4,048 households, a response rate of 62.5 per cent of valid addresses contacted; once again the Electoral Register was the sampling frame and the responses were reweighted to accord with the Labour Force Survey in terms of key household characteristics. Results from this survey on the extent of household poverty have been published in Callan *et al* (1996), which also contains a comprehensive description of the survey itself. We will provide more details of the information obtained in the survey at the relevant points throughout this study. Since the 1994 survey, the same sample of households has been reinterviewed each year by the ESRI, as part of the ECHP Survey. The data this gathers will in the near future provide a basis for an updated profile of poverty in Ireland up to 1997. For the present, however, we concentrate on analysis of the position up to the mid-1990s.

Outline of the Study

Our focus in the next two chapters is on households, the risk of poverty facing households of different types, and in particular the position of those headed by a woman rather than by a man or couple (defined more precisely below). The objective is to analyse how the risk of poverty has changed over the period between 1987 and 1994, and identify the factors which have produced a significant increase in the risk facing households headed by a woman. Chapter 2 presents an overview of trends in poverty risk, then discusses factors which may be expected to influence poverty risk, how these have evolved over the period, and how they would affect female-headed households in particular. Chapter 3 then employs the more formal techniques of regression analysis to identify the key factors at work over the period.

Chapter 4 looks at the poverty risk facing individual adult men and women and how this changed between 1987 and 1994. While the focus is now on the individual, the identification of those who are poor versus non-poor is still on the basis of the income of the household of which they are members. We then bring together these results with those of Chapters 2 and 3, to inform a discussion of how best to develop a system of classifying households that goes beyond characteristics of the "household head", and captures the main factors responsible for differences across households in poverty risk.

Chapter 5 focuses on women in employment. It outlines overall trends in women's participation in the paid labour force and analyses the extent to which women's earnings fall below commonly used low pay benchmarks. It then looks at how many of the women who are low paid also live in poor households, and the contribution which low-paid women's earnings make to keeping households out of poverty. The impact of unemployment versus employment on psychological distress levels for women is examined and compared with the position for men. Finally, policy issues around the obstacles facing women who want to take up paid employment are discussed.

Chapter 6 focuses on the distribution of resources and living standards within the household, and the implications of any disparities in living standards between household members for poverty. Conventional methods of analysis of poverty and income inequality take the household or the narrower family as the income recipient unit, and assume resources are shared so that each individual in a given household/family has the same standard of living. Women's poverty within households with incomes above the poverty line could then be hidden, as could the extent to which women within poor households disproportionately suffer the consequences in terms of reduced consumption. Chapter 6 employs data on non-monetary indicators of deprivation to directly measure deprivation at the level of the individual. As well as analysing differences between spouses, it also looks at the role which household, narrower family and individual incomes play in influencing individual deprivation levels.

Chapter 7 brings together the conclusions of the study and discusses their implications for policy and for future research.

Chapter 2

THE POVERTY RISK OF
FEMALE-HEADED HOUSEHOLDS

Introduction

As outlined in the introductory chapter, in 1987 female-headed households faced a similar risk to other households of being poor, but the risk of poverty for female-headed households had risen significantly by 1994 (Callan, Nolan, *et al*, 1996). The central objective of this chapter is to analyse what happened to poverty over this period in greater depth in order to understand what produced that trend. As is conventional in this type of study, we will be focusing on poverty risk and incidence, so it is important to define these terms at the outset. Suppose one applies a particular poverty standard, and distinguishes different groups or categories of household (on whatever basis). The risk of poverty for a particular group is then the percentage of households in that group that are poor. The incidence of poverty, on the other hand, is the percentage of all poor households coming from the group in question.

The chapter first presents an overview of trends in poverty risk for different types of household. It then discusses factors that may be expected to influence poverty risk, and how they evolved over the period. Finally the chapter summarises the conclusions, which guide the more formal regression analysis to be presented in Chapter 3.

The Overall Pattern 1987–1994

We begin by looking at the risk and incidence of poverty for households of different types. The focus here on the structure of the household with reference to the "household head", and the concept and identification of the household head is central to our discussion, so it requires some discussion at this point. The concept of the household head or household reference person is conventionally adopted in household surveys and their analysis, for convenience and tractability. The way in which that individual is identified varies. For example, in the Household Budget Survey or the Census of Population, (CSO, 1997) does not give an explicit instruction as to who is to be taken as the head of household. It is left to respondents to determine who is the appropriate person. The CSO report that the person whom the household regards as its head is "generally the person who either owns the accommodation or in whose name it is being rented" (CSO, 1997, p. 207). The accommodation may of course be owned or rented by a couple.

The responses to the 1987 and 1994 surveys indicate that, in more than 90 per cent of cases where the head in this sense is a couple, the respondent identifies the male partner as head. In the context of the European Community Household Panel, Eurostat identifies the household reference person explicitly as the owner or tenant of the accommodation, but in cases where two persons are equally responsible for the accommodation specifies that the older of the two be used as the reference person. This will of course also usually be the male in a couple, but does not leave the choice up to the household. While leaving the choice to respondents can be seen as having some advantages, it is problematic in that there is no way of knowing on what basis the choice has been made, and it may itself depend on which household member happens to be interviewed first.

We will return in Chapter 4 to the issue of whether there is a more satisfactory way to categorise households than on the basis of characteristics of the "head" or reference person. In this chapter, our priority is to investigate in greater depth earlier findings on the trends in poverty when households are categorised this way, in particular insofar as they affect households "headed" by women. It is, however, important to set out precisely what this means. As in Callan and Wren (1994) and Callan *et al* (1996), we distinguish three distinct household types: households headed by a couple, households where the head is a "single" man, and households where the head is a "single" woman — where "single" includes widowed, divorced or separated, as well as never married. This means that female-headed households are those where the person owning or renting the accommodation is a woman who does not have a partner in the household.

Table 2.1 shows the risk and incidence of poverty in 1987 and 1994 for households in the ESRI samples for those years, distinguishing these household types. Among households headed by a couple we have further distinguished those without children living in the household and those with children (of any age) in the household. Couple households may have other individuals living in the household as well, such as a parent of one of the partners. Among households headed by a single man or woman we have further distinguished one-person households, lone parent households and others. Lone parents are where the "head" is not living with a spouse or partner but is living with his or her own children of any age. (As with the couple households, there may be other individuals living in the household as well — such as a brother or sister of the lone parent, or the children's grandparent.) "Others" then comprise households where the head or reference person is living with others but not his or her children: these consist of unrelated persons (such as a group of young people) or related persons (most often brothers and/or sisters) sharing accommodation.

We see from Table 2.1 that, first of all, the sample is dominated by households headed by a couple. These accounted for 69 per cent of all households in 1987, but had dropped to 62 per cent by 1994. In both years, over three-quarters of couple households had children of the couple living in the household as well. Households consisting of an adult living alone accounted for 17 per cent of the sample in 1987, but this was up to 22 per cent by 1994 – and in slightly more than half of these the adult was a woman. Male lone parent households were very rare in both years, accounting for less than two per cent of all households. Female lone parent households increased from seven to 10 per cent of all households. The "other" category accounted for about five per cent of all households in both years, and is fairly evenly divided between those where the head is male and those where the head is female.

TABLE 2.1: RISK AND INCIDENCE OF POVERTY BY WHETHER FEMALE HEAD AND HOUSEHOLD TYPE IN 1987 AND 1994

	1987			1994		
	% below 50% line	*% of Poor House-holds*	*% of Sample House-holds*	*% below 50% line*	*% of Poor House-holds*	*% of Sample House-holds*
Couple households						
Couple, no children	11.4	8.5	12.2	10.6	7.5	13.3
Couple with children	18.9	66.2	57.0	18.6	47.6	48.2
Male head						
One person	22.5	9.9	7.2	20.7	11.8	10.7
Lone parent	17.3	1.8	1.7	11.4	0.9	1.5
Other	15.6	3.3	3.5	6.3	0.9	2.8
Female head						
One person	3.8	2.2	9.4	24.4	14.6	11.3
Lone parent	17.4	7.6	7.1	31.7	16.5	9.8
Other	3.2	0.4	2.0	1.0	0.1	2.4
All households						
One person	11.9	12.1	16.6	22.6	26.5	22.0
Couple, no children	11.4	8.5	12.2	10.6	7.5	13.3
Couple with children	18.9	66.2	57.0	18.6	47.6	48.2
Lone parent	17.3	9.4	8.8	29.0	17.4	11.3
Other	11.1	3.7	5.4	3.8	1.1	5.2

The first and fourth columns of Table 2.1 show the poverty *risk* for households of different types in 1987 and 1994, respectively.[1] Here we use the 50 per cent relative income poverty line, and the equivalence scale which uses a "weight" of 1 for the first adult,

---

[1] Minor revisions in data and weights mean that there are slight differences between the poverty risks reported here and those in Callan *et al* (1996).

0.66 for each other adult, and 0.33 for each child in the household. The following can be seen as important trends in the risk of poverty over the period:

- The poverty risk remained substantially unchanged for couple households between 1987 and 1994. The risk is higher for couples with children (about 19 per cent) than it is for couples without children (about 11 per cent).

- The poverty risk for women living alone increased substantially between 1987 and 1994, from four per cent to 24 per cent. In 1987 women living alone were much less likely than men living alone to be poor, but by 1994 the risk was slightly higher for these women (24 per cent) than for men (21 per cent).

- In 1987 lone parent households faced roughly the same risk of poverty as couples with children, and there was no difference between male and female lone parents. By 1994, however, the risk had increased sharply for female lone parents who were household heads.

Next, the second and fifth columns of Table 2.1 show the *incidence* of poverty for each household type — the proportion of all poor households that fall into each of the categories. Incidence will be a function of the total number of households of this type in the population, and of the risk of poverty faced by different types of household. Most poor households are couple households in both periods, because this is the most common household type, but with the proportion falling between 1987 and 1994. In 1987 about two thirds of poor households consisted of couples with children, and a further nine per cent consisted of couples without children. By 1994, couples with children accounted for just under half of all poor households, while couples without children made up an additional eight per cent of poor households.

Individuals living alone made up about 12 per cent of poor households in 1987, but this had more than doubled to about 26 per cent by 1994. In the earlier period, most of the poor living alone were men, but by 1994 slightly more than half were women. As we saw earlier, the increase in the incidence of poverty among one-person households was driven mainly by the increased risk of poverty faced by women living alone. Only about one poor household in ten in 1987 was headed by a lone parent. By 1994, this had increased to about 18 per cent. The increase, again, resulted mainly from the increase in risk faced by households headed by a female lone parent.

Overall, then, when we look at different household types it is clear that the changes in poverty risk between 1987 and 1994 reflect a worsening situation for households headed by a woman. In the following sections we will explore the factors responsible for this change. We first present in the remainder of this chapter an overview of the factors to be considered and how they evolved over the period, before turning in Chapter 3 to a more formal regression analysis.

Factors Influencing the Risk of Poverty

In the main, female-headed households are made up of women living alone and lone parents, as we saw in Table 2.1. We have already seen in the previous section that both of these groups have a higher risk of poverty than households headed by a couple. The risk of poverty for women living alone rose from a low initial rate in 1987 to a rate that is somewhat higher than that for men living alone by 1994, and the poverty risk for female lone parents also increased substantially in this period.

There are a number of possible reasons why the risk of poverty might have increased for women living alone:

- Young single women may have become more likely to move to independent accommodation at an earlier stage. The gap in poverty risk between single men and women in 1987 and the narrowing of this gap by 1994 suggests that the living arrangements of young men and women may be becoming more similar.

- Older single women with low incomes may have become less likely to share accommodation with relatives (such as a brother or sister).

- Widowed women may have become more likely to live alone than with grown children.

- Marital breakdown may have led to an increase in the number of separated or divorced women with low incomes living alone.

All of these patterns assume a change in the trend of living arrangements, which leads to smaller household sizes. If, for example, a young woman who is unemployed or has low earnings switches from living with her widowed mother on a widow's non-contributory pension to living alone, the result might be two poor households rather than a single non-poor household.

In the case of female lone parents, we may have a similar set of changes in living arrangements and relationships that underlie the risk of poverty:

- A greater proportion of lone parent households may consist of unmarried or separated/divorced women with children, with a higher risk of poverty than those consisting of older, often widowed women with adult children.

- The proportion of older (usually widowed) mothers who have adult children in the household may be reduced if adult children leave home earlier, so that widows become more likely to be living alone or with dependent children only.

We can now list in Table 2.2 the factors that we would expect to have an impact on the poverty risk of female-headed households, and how they will be incorporated into the regression models to be analysed in the next chapter. In that analysis the focus is on non-couple households and the point of comparison will be households headed by a male. We know at the outset that female-headed households face a higher risk of poverty in 1994 than in 1987. The analysis will explore whether this increased risk is accounted for by differences with respect to factors such as living arrangements and labour force participation.

Female Versus Male Head

The sex of the household head is the first factor to be taken into account. It is measured in the regression model via a dummy variable where households headed by a woman are given a value of 1 and those headed by a man (not by a couple) are given the value 0.

TABLE 2.2: LIST OF FACTORS INFLUENCING RISK OF POVERTY FOR
NON-COUPLE HOUSEHOLDS

Head is female versus male

Number of adults in household

Number of children (age under 18) in household

Age of head

Marital status of head

   ◊   Separated/divorced

   ◊   Widowed

   ◊   Never married

Household type

   ◊   One person

   ◊   Lone parent and children (with or without other persons)

   ◊   Other household type (non-relatives; siblings; etc.)

Life cycle stage

   ◊   Pre-family (age under 45, no children in household)

   ◊   Youngest child age 0–4

   ◊   Youngest child 5–9

   ◊   Youngest child 10–17

   ◊   Youngest child 18+

   ◊   Post-family (age over 45, no children in household)

Labour force status of head

   ◊   Head at work for pay

   ◊   Head unemployed

   ◊   Head retired

   ◊   Head engaged on home duties

   ◊   Head in other economic status

Social class of head

   ◊   Professional/managerial (1 and 2)

   ◊   Other non-manual (Social class 3)

   ◊   Skilled manual (Social class 4)

   ◊   Semi-skilled manual (Social class 5)

   ◊   Unskilled manual (Social class 6)

   ◊   Social class unknown (Social class 7)

Number of other adults at work

Number of other adults unemployed

Number of Adults and Children

The next characteristics to be considered are the number of adults (individuals over age 18) and the number of children (under 18) in the household (not necessarily children of the household head). Since children add to the "needs" of the household without adding to its income, we would expect that, all other things being equal, a greater number of children would be associated with an increased risk of poverty. This difference in "needs" is incorporated into the equivalence scale used in deriving the poverty status of the household. The equivalence scale used here gives the first adult in the household a weight of 1; subsequent adults (age 14 and over) are given a weight of 0.66 and children (age under 14) are given a weight of 0.33.[2]

The equivalence scale counts as children those under 14 since we would expect the resource needs of a 15–17 year-old to be closer to those of an adult than of a younger child, whereas in looking at factors predicting poverty, we count under-18s since most in the 15–17 age range will not be contributing to household income.

Additional adults increase a household's need for income, but they also have the potential to add to the household's income through income from employment or social welfare transfers.

Table 2.3 shows the average number of adults and the average number of children in different household types in 1987 and 1994. Households headed by a couple with children unsurprisingly have more adults than lone parent households, but the gap between them had increased by 1994 because the average number of adults in female lone parent households fell. By 1994, female lone parent households with children had fewer adults, on average, than any of the other households consisting of adults and children. House-holds consisting of couples and children have an average of two children, whereas lone parent households have one on average. However, for female lone parent households, that average in-creased from 0.9 in 1987 to 1.3 in 1994. There was virtually no change in average size over the period for households consisting of couples without children.

---

[2] This is equivalence scale "A" described in Callan, *et al* (1996), p. 65.

TABLE 2.3: AVERAGE NUMBERS OF ADULTS AND CHILDREN BY
WHETHER FEMALE HEAD AND HOUSEHOLD TYPE IN 1987 AND 1994

	1987		1994	
	Average number adults	*Average number children*	*Average number adults*	*Average number children*
Couple households				
Couple, no children	2.03	0.02	2.03	0.00
Couple with children	2.66	2.02	2.75	1.98
Male head				
One person	1.00	0.00	1.00	0.00
Lone parent	2.24	0.69	2.24	0.70
Other	2.61	0.23	2.32	0.08
Female head				
One person	1.00	0.00	1.00	0.00
Lone parent	2.28	0.93	1.98	1.32
Other	2.56	0.10	2.30	0.07
All households				
One person	1.00	0.00	1.00	0.00
Couple, no children	2.03	0.02	2.03	0.00
Couple with children	2.66	2.02	2.75	1.98
Lone parent	2.27	0.89	2.01	1.24
Other	2.59	0.18	2.31	0.07

Life-Cycle Stage

The life-cycle stage of the household is likely to influence poverty
risk for a number of reasons, including its implications for labour
force participation of household members. When children are
young, the mother may have fewer hours available to work in paid
employment. As children grow older, they themselves begin to
earn prior to setting up households in their own right. The summary measure of life-cycle stage used here is based on the age of
the youngest child of the household head, or on the age of the
head (or female partner in couple households) for households
where the head does not have children living in the household.

The age groups of children are the pre-school years (age under five), age five to 10, age 10 to 17 and age 18 and over. Households where the head has no children and is under age 45 are considered "pre-family" households, while those where the head is over age 45 are "post-family" households. There is a certain arbitrariness involved in the choice of this age cut-off, but the majority of those regarded as pre-family are under 35 and the majority of those regarded as post-family are over 55, so the exact choice of year would not make much difference.

We see from Table 2.4 that the main changes in composition of the sample between 1987 and 1994 were a decline in the proportion of households where the youngest child is under age four, and increases in the proportion of households where the head is at the pre-family or the post-family life cycle-stage. The drop in households with young children mainly affected couple households, while the increases in pre- and post-family households mainly involved the non-couple households.

This life-cycle classification is then seen to capture a considerable amount of variation in poverty risk. In both years, the risk was lowest for pre-family households and households with at least one grown-up child still living at home. There was a shift in the relative position of these two groups, however, with pre-family households having the lowest risk of poverty in 1987, and those containing grown children having the lowest risk in 1994. In fact, the risk increased slightly in this period for pre-family households, and decreased slightly for households with grown children. The low risk of poverty for households with grown children was true in 1994 for households headed by couples, by males and by females.

The risk of poverty was highest in both years in households with children under 18 — with a tendency for the risk to be greatest for households with younger children — and rose over the period. The risk is substantially higher for female lone parent households than for couple households, however; and for that group the increase over the period from 1987 to 1994 was particularly marked. Post-family couple households occupied an intermediate position in terms of poverty risk in both periods, but the risk of poverty faced by post-family female-headed households increased substantially between 1987 and 1994.

TABLE 2.4: RISK AND INCIDENCE OF POVERTY BY WHETHER FEMALE HEAD AND LIFE-CYCLE STAGE IN 1987 AND 1994*

	1987			1994		
	% below 50% line	% of Poor Households	% of Sample Households	% below 50% line	% of Poor Households	% of Sample Households
Couple						
Pre-family	6.9	1.4	3.3	4.9	1.0	4.0
Youngest child 0–4	22.6	34.1	24.6	23.8	21.0	16.6
Youngest child 5–9	21.1	12.7	9.8	23.0	11.5	9.4
Youngest child 10–17	18.8	15.0	13.0	19.0	13.1	13.0
Youngest child 18+	7.5	4.5	9.7	4.1	2.0	9.3
Post-family	13.0	7.2	9.0	13.1	6.5	9.3
Male						
Pre-family	6.8	1.4	3.3	12.1	3.1	4.8
Youngest child 0–4	----*	----*	0.0	0.0	0.0	0.0
Youngest child 5–9	73.4	0.7	0.1	0.0	0.0	0.1
Youngest child 10–17	7.3	0.2	0.4	45.8	0.7	0.3
Youngest child 18+	14.8	1.0	1.1	3.9	0.2	1.1
Post-family	26.3	11.9	7.3	20.8	9.7	8.8

	1987			1994		
	% below 50% line	% of Poor Households	% of Sample Households	% below 50% line	% of Poor Households	% of Sample Households
Female						
Pre-family	0.0	0.0	1.6	9.7	1.4	2.7
Youngest child 0–4	34.1	1.8	0.9	59.9	5.3	1.7
Youngest child 5–9	29.5	0.9	0.5	55.8	3.6	1.2
Youngest child 10–17	31.4	2.8	1.4	43.0	5.8	2.5
Youngest child 18+	7.8	2.1	4.3	7.5	1.7	4.3
Post-family	4.3	2.6	9.7	22.8	13.4	11.0
All						
Pre-family	5.5	2.8	8.2	9.0	5.5	11.5
Youngest child 0–4	23.0	35.9	25.4	27.0	26.3	18.3
Youngest child 5–9	22.2	14.2	10.4	26.6	15.1	10.7
Youngest child 10–17	19.7	17.9	14.8	23.3	19.6	15.8
Youngest child 18+	8.1	7.6	15.1	5.1	4.0	14.7
Post-family	13.5	21.6	26.0	19.1	29.5	29.0

* Broken lines (-----) indicate that there were too few cases in the sample to provide a reliable estimate.

Age

Age and life-cycle stage are closely related, but age is also included in the model as a continuous variable. As shown in Table
2.5, in 1994 younger households (where the head is under 30)
faced the highest risk of poverty and older ones (aged 65 or over)
the lowest risk. However, this varies across household types. For
couple households, there was a consistent decline in the risk of
poverty with age, whereas in 1987 the only variation had been the
relatively low poverty rate for the elderly. For female-headed
households, poverty rates increased for all age groups between
1987 and 1994 and were then highest for those aged 30-44. The
age pattern for male-headed households is different: in both years,
the risk of poverty is by far the highest for the 45 to 64 age group
with a sharp drop after retirement age.

Marital Status

The marital status categories for non-couple households distinguish between household heads who are divorced or separated,
widowed, and never married. Although the number of cases where
the household head is divorced or separated is small (12 per cent
of all non-couple households), the inclusion of this variable in the
model will allow us to assess the extent to which marital breakdown has implications for poverty risk. In general, among those
receiving social welfare transfers we might expect widowed
individuals to have a lower risk of poverty than never-married
individuals to the extent that they are entitled to non-means
tested Survivor's Benefit payments, which they may receive in
addition to any income from employment. Table 2.6 shows the
marital status for household heads living alone and those who
were lone parents in the 1987 and 1994 samples.

We see that among one-person households, men living alone
are most likely to have never married, while women living alone
are most likely to be widowed. There was a substantial increase in
the proportion of women living alone who never married over the
period, suggesting that young single women were more likely to
set up independent households by 1994. Turning to lone parents,
while the proportion of male lone parents who were separated or

TABLE 2.5: RISK AND INCIDENCE OF POVERTY BY WHETHER FEMALE HEAD AND AGE GROUP OF HEAD IN 1987 AND 1994

	1987			1994		
	% below 50% line	*% of Poor Households*	*% of Sample Households*	*% below 50% line*	*% of Poor Households*	*% of Sample Households*
Couple						
Under 30	19.4	8.6	7.2	24.7	6.2	4.7
30-44	19.6	33.8	28.0	19.7	25.6	24.4
45-64	17.3	25.5	24.0	15.0	18.8	23.6
65+	11.2	6.8	9.9	9.6	4.5	8.8
Male						
Under 30	6.4	0.3	0.8	6.2	0.6	1.7
30-44	8.6	1.4	2.6	14.5	2.5	3.2
45-64	37.4	11.2	4.9	34.3	8.4	4.6
65+	8.8	2.2	4.0	7.5	2.2	5.5

	1987			1994		
	% below 50% line	% of Poor Households	% of Sample Households	% below 50% line	% of Poor Households	% of Sample Households
Female						
Under 30	16.0	1.2	1.2	34.8	5.0	2.7
30-44	20.7	3.0	2.3	39.9	8.7	4.1
45-64	11.5	4.1	5.8	27.0	8.7	6.1
65+	3.5	2.0	9.2	15.5	8.7	10.6
All						
Under 30	17.8	10.1	9.2	24.3	11.8	9.1
30-44	18.8	38.1	33.0	21.8	36.8	31.7
45-64	19.2	40.8	34.7	19.7	36.0	34.3
65+	7.7	11.0	23.1	11.7	15.5	24.9

divorced doubled from eight to 16 per cent between the two years, widowhood remains by far the most common marital status. None of the male lone parents in our sample were never married. The major change for female lone parents was the large increase in the proportion who had never married, although the proportion who were separated or divorced also increased, while the proportion who were widowed dropped substantially. To the extent that widowhood is associated with a lower risk of poverty for lone parents than never having married or being separated, then, this could potentially account for a substantial proportion of the increased risk of poverty for female lone parents between 1987 and 1994.

TABLE 2.6: MARITAL STATUS OF HEAD BY SEX FOR ADULTS LIVING ALONE AND LONE PARENTS, 1987 AND 1994

	1987		1994	
	One Person	*Lone Parent*	*One Person*	*Lone Parent*
	%	%	%	%
Male				
Separated/divorced	9.4	7.8	7.8	16.3
Widowed	21.1	92.2	19.6	83.7
Never Married	69.4	0.0	72.5	0.0
	100.0	100.0	100.0	100.0
Female				
Separated/divorced	3.7	25.0	3.9	30.7
Widowed	67.4	68.5	55.6	47.2
Never Married	29.0	6.5	40.5	22.1
	100.0	100.0	100.0	100.0

Economic Status and Social Class

In previous research on poverty in Ireland and elsewhere the economic status of the household head was found to be a major predictor of poverty status. In particular, where the head is unemployed or ill/disabled the risk of poverty is generally high. In addition, though, between 1987 and 1994 the poverty risk of households where the head is engaged in what is conventionally termed in labour force categorisations "home duties" — in other words working full-time in the home — has been seen to have

increased substantially (Callan *et al* 1996, p. 96). Table 2.7 shows
the poverty status of households of different types according to the
labour force status of the household head.[3] (In couple households,
the labour force status of the male partner is shown in this table;
in the next chapter, we will look in more detail at the impact of
women's paid work on the poverty risk of couple households.)

For couple households and households headed by men, the
greatest risk of poverty is faced by those where the head is unemployed. This pattern held true in both 1987 and 1994, with the risk
of poverty for couple households with an unemployed head increasing slightly while it remained substantially the same for male-
headed households. Households with unemployed female heads
faced a lower poverty risk, but account for less than one per cent of
sample households. Overall, households with an unemployed head
accounted for about one-third of poor households in both years.

Households headed by someone who is ill or disabled faced a
relatively high risk and a substantial increase in the risk of poverty between 1987 and 1994. Among female-headed households,
this is the household type that faces the highest risk of poverty in
1994. Overall, however, because the proportion of households
headed by someone who is ill or disabled is low, these households
account for a relatively small proportion of all poor households.

While the risk of poverty faced by households headed by a
woman working full-time in the home is not as high as that faced
by households with an unemployed or disabled head, it rose from
10 to 37 per cent between 1987 and 1994, and was then about
twice the overall poverty rate. Because a substantial proportion of
all households in 1994 were headed by a woman engaged in home
duties, such households accounted for over one in four poor
households in 1994, a dramatic increase on the figure of under
seven per cent in 1987. What Table 2.7 also brings out is that the
risk of poverty is very low where the head is at work, particularly
where the head is an employee. Thus among female-headed
households where the head is an employee, the poverty risk is
only three per cent.

---

[3] Once again there are slight differences between some of the figures presented here and in Callan *et al* (1996) due to minor revisions to data and
weights.

TABLE 2.7: RISK AND INCIDENCE OF POVERTY BY WHETHER FEMALE HEAD AND LABOUR FORCE (LF) STATUS OF HEAD IN 1987 AND 1994*

	1987			1994		
	% below 50% line	% of Poor Households	% of Sample Households	% below 50% line	% of Poor Households	% of Sample Households
Couple — LF Status Head						
Employee	3.5	6.9	31.8	3.5	5.4	28.7
Self-employed	9.9	4.2	6.8	16.7	6.6	7.4
Farmer	33.6	17.0	8.2	22.8	6.9	5.6
Unemployed	57.7	33.4	9.4	61.4	26.1	8.0
Ill/Disabled	31.3	8.0	4.2	42.4	4.5	2.0
Retired	9.3	4.9	8.5	10.8	5.4	9.5
Home Duties	17.8	0.2	0.1	0	0	0.1
Other	-----*	-----*	0	18.9	0.2	0.2
Male — LF Status Head						
Employee	0.0	0.0	2.7	0	0	4.2
Self-employed	22.2	0.7	0.5	0	0	0.7
Farmer	28.0	5.9	3.4	16.8	1.9	2.2
Unemployed	64.6	3.6	0.9	63.9	5.2	1.5
Ill/Disabled	26.9	2.1	1.3	60.7	3.1	1.0
Retired	12.5	2.6	3.4	12.2	3.5	5.3

Home Duties	0	0	0	39.3	0.1	0
Other	-----	-----	0	0	0	0.1
Female— LF Status Head						
Employee	4.1	0.9	3.4	2.8	0.6	4.3
Self-employed	0.0	0	0.2	0	0	0.4
Farmer	29.4	1.2	0.7	0	0	0.4
Unemployed	17.8	0.3	0.3	26.6	0.8	0.6
Ill/Disabled	19.2	0.6	0.5	50.7	1.8	0.7
Retired	4.1	0.6	2.5	9.5	1.8	3.5
Home Duties	9.8	6.5	10.9	36.8	26.2	13.4
Other	-----	-----	0	0	0	0.1
All — LF Status Head						
Employee	3.6	7.8	38.0	3.4	6.0	37.2
Self-employed	11.2	4.8	7.5	15.8	6.6	8.6
Farmer	44.0	24.1	12.3	27.2	8.8	8.2
Unemployed	62.6	37.4	10.6	70.4	32.0	10.1
Ill/Disabled	37.5	10.7	6.0	66.4	9.4	3.6
Retired	12.0	8.1	14.5	15.4	10.7	18.3
Home Duties	9.9	6.7	11.1	36.7	26.3	13.5
Other	-----	-----	0.1	11.2	0.2	0.4

* Broken lines (-----) indicate that there were too few cases in the sample to provide a reliable estimate.

Social Class

To distinguish households by social class we employ the Central Statistics Office social class categories, based on the occupation (or previous occupation) of the household head or reference person. Farmers are assigned to the different social class categories based on the acreage farmed. Social class 1 includes higher level professional and managerial occupations such as engineers, managers, accountants, and doctors. Social class 2 includes lower level professional and managerial occupations, many of which are dominated by women, such as teachers and nurses, as well as building contractors without employees and hotel or restaurant managers. Social class 3 includes most routine non-manual occupations such as clerical workers, typists, bookkeepers, cashiers, chefs and cooks and computing machine operators. Social class 4 includes the skilled manual jobs such as carpenter/joiner, electrician, fitters and fishermen. Social class 5 includes semi-skilled manual occupations such as most production jobs in factories, shop assistants, waiter/waitress, bar attendants. Social class 6 includes unskilled manual occupations such as labourers and domestic and related workers (chambermaid, nanny, housekeeper, kitchen porter, and washer-up).

We include a separate category (which we label category 7) for cases where the social class is unknown. This often arises where the individual has never worked in paid employment, which may be true of many of the women in the sample, as well as of young people who are still in full-time education. This group is included as a separate category rather than omitting them from the analysis. We would expect the risk of poverty to increase as we move from the higher level professional and managerial social class to the unskilled social class.

Numbers at Work / Unemployed

The economic status of other adults in the household is also considered by including measures of the number of other adults (besides the household head) who are at work in paid employment, and the number who are unemployed. We would expect the numbers at work to reduce poverty risk, and the numbers unemployed to increase poverty risk. The impact of these factors may be smaller than the head's economic status, however, since "other adults" are often younger people in the household who are likely to have lower earnings.

TABLE 2.8: AVERAGE NUMBERS WORKING FOR PAY AND UNEMPLOYED BY WHETHER FEMALE HEAD AND HOUSEHOLD TYPE IN 1987 AND 1994

	1987		1994	
	Average no. at work	*Average no. unemployed*	*Average no. at work*	*Average no. unemployed*
Couple Households				
Couple, no children	0.68	0.09	0.82	0.05
Couple with children	1.34	0.34	1.42	0.28
Male Head				
One person	0.45	0.11	0.44	0.10
Lone parent	1.09	0.40	1.08	0.42
Other	1.33	0.11	0.98	0.16
Female Head				
One person	0.18	0.01	0.20	0.03
Lone parent	0.97	0.38	0.56	0.37
Other	1.70	0.14	1.29	0.08
All Households — Household Type				
One person	0.30	0.05	0.32	0.06
Couple, no children	0.68	0.09	0.82	0.05
Couple with children	1.34	0.34	1.42	0.28
Lone parent	0.99	0.38	0.63	0.38
Other	1.46	0.12	1.13	0.12

Table 2.8 shows the average numbers working for pay and the average numbers unemployed for different household types. Of the major household types, couples with children tend to have the highest average number of persons working for pay, at 1.4. Fewer

than half of male one-person households and about one-fifth of women living alone are working for pay, with little change between 1987 and 1994. Male and female lone parent households had approximately the same number of adults at work on average in 1987. By 1994, however, a substantial gap had emerged, with the average number at work remaining stable at 1.8 for male-headed households, but dropping substantially to 0.6 in female-headed households.

Conclusions

This chapter has described overall trends in the risk of poverty for households of different types between 1987 and 1994, bringing out in particular the increasing risk over the period for female-headed households. It then looked at a range of factors that might be expected to influence the risk of poverty for households, and also described how the major ones evolved over the period. By 1994, lone mother households had fewer adults on average, a higher average number of children and a sizeable drop in the proportion of lone mothers who were widowed rather than never married or divorced/separated compared to their situation in 1987. Women living alone were also more likely by 1994 to be single than widowed. The next part of the analysis draws on these results to inform a more formal regression analysis, aimed at identifying with greater precision which aspects of household structure or characteristics of individuals most substantially influence risk of poverty.

Chapter 3

REGRESSION ANALYSIS OF POVERTY RISKS

Introduction

Our aim in this chapter, building on the results of Chapter 2, is to use what are known as logistic regression models to identify those aspects of household structure or characteristics of individuals that most substantially influence risk of poverty. This allows us to home in on those factors which have the greatest impact on the risk of poverty facing female-headed households, and in particular what changes between 1987 and 1994 drove the observed increase in overall risk for those households. In the next chapter, the regression results are also used to inform the discussion of how best to classify households so as to distinguish them on the basis of the most important factors which actually contribute to poverty risk.

Methods

It may be useful at the outset to provide a brief description of the statistical methods to be employed in this chapter. Logit regression models provide a suitable methodology for the identification of those aspects of household structure or characteristics of individuals that most substantially influence risk of poverty. A logit regression model is used to predict a dependent variable (poverty in this case) which has a number of categories (poor and not poor) rather than being measured on a continuum (such as income). The coefficients in the models we develop here show the impact of each explanatory variable on the (log of the) odds of being under the 50 per cent poverty line. The logic is very similar to that of ordinary least squares multiple regression analysis, which is often used to analyse continuous variables such as income or hours worked. The models allow us to isolate the effects on poverty risk of different characteristics of the household such as age of the head, number of children, or whether the head is working for pay.

The following are some key questions that can be addressed using the logit regression model:

- To what extent are the differences in poverty risk between female-headed households and other households due to differences in household composition?

- When differences in living arrangements (such as living alone, living in a household headed by a lone parent) and in labour force participation are controlled, are households headed by women still poorer than households headed by men?

- In couple households, do the characteristics of the female partner (e.g. whether she is working) help explain poverty when characteristics of the male partner are taken into account?

The analysis of the changing situation between 1987 and 1994 which follows is divided into two main sections:

- The poverty risk of non-couple households

- The poverty risk of couple households.

We first compare and investigate the situation of non-couple households headed by women versus those headed by men. This is central to the concerns of the study because — with equal numbers of men and women in couple households by definition — the difference in poverty rates between men and women will be driven by differences between these male and female-headed households. Going on to look at couple households, the question on which we focus is the extent to which the characteristics of the female head of household matter in understanding the poverty risk of these households.

Modelling Poverty for Non-couple Households in 1994

So far, we have seen that the risk of poverty tends to be greater for households headed by women than for those headed by men or couples and that the difference increased in magnitude between 1987 and 1994. We have also identified some of the factors associated with a greater risk of poverty at the household level: female, younger heads in households with fewer adults and more children where the head is not working for pay have a higher risk of poverty. At this point, we turn to logit models to disentangle the effects of factors such as life-cycle stage, household composition and labour force participation on poverty risk for both years. Once we have established this for 1994, we can move on to discover what changes between 1987 and 1994 were primarily responsible for the increase in risk faced by households headed by women.

Table A3.1[1] shows the set of logit models for non-couple households in 1994. The dependent variable is the log odds of poverty (using the 50 per cent poverty line) for the household. (The overall risk of poverty for all non-couple households was 22 per cent.) Model 1 is the base model with no independent variables added. Model 2 adds the sex and age of the household head, and household composition (the number of children and adults in the household). We see that even controlling for age and household composition, households headed by women have a higher poverty risk, as indicated by the positive coefficient for female heads. Increasing age and a greater number of adults is associated with reduced poverty risk, while the risk increases with the number of children in the household.

In Model 3 we add the household type variables. The omitted or comparison group is individuals who live alone. Lone parent households experience a higher risk of poverty than those living alone, while the "other" household type does not differ significantly from one-person households.

The next model adds two life-cycle stage variables: pre-family households and households where the youngest child is over 18.

---

[1] See Appendix, p. 133.

The comparison group is post-family households.[2] Pre-family households have a lower risk of poverty than post-family households when one controls for the other factors in the model, but those with grown-up children are not significantly different from the comparison group. Two other features worth noting in this model are that the poverty risk of female-headed households *per se* is now no longer significantly greater than that of male-headed households; and that the poverty risk of lone parent households is not significantly greater than that of one-person households. The number of children in the household is not statistically significant in this model. This probably reflects the fact that there is only a small amount of variation in the number of children for non-couple households, and that much of the variation associated with the presence of children is being captured by the variable for pre-family households. It appears then, that the greater risk of poverty of female-headed households versus male-headed households in 1994 is associated with the household composition and life-cycle stage of these households. Model 5 adds the marital status of the household head, with the omitted group being those who never married. The effect of marital status is not statistically significant, although the negative sign is in the expected direction (reduced risk) for widowhood.

In the remaining models we explore the role of economic status and social class in accounting for poverty risk. In Model 6 we add three variables for the economic status of the household head. The comparison groups are those engaged on home duties, ill/disabled or in other economic statuses (most often in education). The coefficients indicate that households where the head is unemployed do not differ significantly from those where the head is engaged in home duties, ill/disabled or in education.[3] However, where the head

---

[2] The variables for households with children could not be added since this would have resulted in multicollinearity in the model. The effect of having children in the household is already captured by the "lone parent" variable and the measure of the number of children in the household.

[3] Another model (not shown) tested whether the risk of poverty for heads engaged in home duties differed from the risk for those in other economic statuses. The risk for heads engaged in home duties did not differ significantly from the risk of those who were unemployed with the other variables in the model controlled.

is working for pay or retired the risk of poverty is considerably lower. Notice also in this model that when we control for economic status, the coefficient for female head becomes negative: if it were not for the differences in economic status between male- and female-headed households, female-headed households would actually face a lower risk of poverty. The coefficient for age of head remains negative, indicating that it is not just whether the head is retired that accounts for the tendency for poverty risk to decline with age.

Model 7 adds the social class of the household head. There is a general tendency for poverty risk to increase as we move from the professional/managerial social classes (the omitted comparison category) to the unskilled social class. However, the difference in risk between the other non-manual category (social class 3) and the higher and lower professional/managerial social classes is not statistically significant.

In Model 8 we add variables reflecting the economic status of other household members. (Remember that we are dealing with non-couple households here, so that none of the other household members is a spouse or partner of the head). The poverty risk decreases with the number of other household members who are working for pay, but the number unemployed does not have a significant impact.

The final model, Model 9, is arrived at by an iterative procedure where the non-significant variables are removed from the model one by one, the remaining coefficients are carefully examined to determine how the pattern is changing, and alternative summary variables are added where appropriate. For instance, the pattern of coefficients for social class suggested that the main distinction in poverty risk was between the manual and non-manual social classes. Similarly, the coefficients for household type suggested that the important contrast was between those living alone and other household types. Consequently, the non-significant coefficients were removed and these two variables were added. The main factors contributing to a reduction in the risk of poverty are the age of the head, the number of adults in the household, being at the pre-family life-cycle stage, widowhood, the head working in paid employment or being retired, the number of other adults in the household working for pay. The factors increasing risk, on the other hand, are being in a manual social class, or living alone. When one controls for these factors, female-headed households actually have a small but statistically significant reduced risk of poverty compared to male-headed (non-couple) households.

The final column of the table shows the expected effect on poverty risk of each factor at the average poverty rate for non-couple households (which we saw is 22 per cent). One feature of logit models is that the effect of any variable depends on the values of all the other variables in the model. In other words, the amount by which a change in one variable would increase or decrease the poverty risk depends on whether the poverty risk is already high or low. If a group of households already has a high risk of poverty, an additional risk factor (such as the main bread-winner being unemployed) will have a smaller impact on the poverty rate than it would if the households had a low risk of poverty. This means that we cannot give a single, easily interpretable figure for the "effect" of a given variable. Since the estimated effect of factors such as unemployment and number of children depend on other aspects of the household, we need to find some way to "standardise" the estimates. The final column in Table A3.1 does this by estimating the effect of each factor on the poverty rate of a group of households with the average level of poverty for all non-couple households.[4] This allows us to assess the relative importance of the different factors.

We can see from the final column that the factors which make the biggest difference are whether the household head is at work or retired rather than in some other economic status, or is at the pre-family life-cycle stage. All three of these factors are associated with a substantial reduction in poverty risk. The next most important factor is whether the individual lives alone, which is associated with a substantial increase in poverty risk. Comparing the sizes of the effects of living alone and of being at the pre-family stage, we can see that pre-family individuals living alone would

---

[4] If we chose to standardise on a group with a higher risk of poverty (say 70 per cent), the effect of the factors which tend to increase poverty risk would be reduced (since the risk is already high, and it would "take more" to push it yet higher) while the effect of those factors which would tend to reduce poverty risk would be greater.

not tend to be poorer than average (the effects would cancel out), but that those over 45 living alone do tend to be poorer, all other things being equal.

Where the head is in one of the three manual social classes (skilled manual, semi-skilled manual and unskilled manual), the risk of poverty is increased. Comparing the size of this coefficient in the final model with that for the head working for pay, we can see that being in a non-manual social class would reduce poverty by about half as much as working for pay, all other things being equal. The effect of having one additional household member at work is about the same magnitude as the social class effect, reducing poverty risk by about half the amount of having the head at work. However, if we are comparing households with no other adult to those with an additional adult who is at work, we need to take account of two effects in the model. We would need to take account of the reduced risk associated with the mere presence of this other adult (nine percentage points in the example) as well as the effect of having one additional adult at work (12 percentage points). When we add these, the reduction in poverty risk for the example case would be 21 percentage points, about the same size as the reduction in poverty risk if the head works for pay.

The final group of variables have smaller but significant effects on poverty risk. The gap between male and female households (which works in favour of female-headed households with these other factors controlled) is about the same size as the gap we would expect between households where the head differs in age by ten years; or where the household has one additional adult, or where the head is widowed. Note that the presence of additional adults is associated with a reduced risk of poverty even when we control for whether the additional adults are working. This probably reflects the fact that other adults may have income from social welfare or pension schemes, even when they do not work for pay.

Table 3.2 provides an alternative presentation of the results from the logit model by predicting the risk of poverty for households in specified circumstances, and varying one factor at a time. For instance, the first row of the table uses the coefficients from the logit model to predict the risk of poverty for a household consisting of a 25-year-old woman who lives alone, has never married, is unemployed and whose usual occupation is in the unskilled manual social class. The predicted poverty rate for this type of case is 52 per cent. Note that since there is no significant difference between those who are unemployed and those engaged in home duties when other factors are controlled, the predicted poverty rate would be about the same for a woman engaged in home duties.

The second row of the table indicates that if the household head was male instead of female, the predicted poverty rate would be 65 per cent rather than 52 per cent. Essentially this means that there are other unmeasured factors, not in the model, which work to increase the risk of poverty for male-headed households. The next row shows that if the woman in our example were widowed rather than unemployed her risk of poverty would be expected to drop to 40 per cent. Next we see that if she was age 67 and retired, or if her age was the same but she worked for pay we would expect a very substantial drop in her risk of poverty to three to four per cent.

TABLE 3.2: PREDICTED RISK OF POVERTY FOR NON-COUPLE HOUSEHOLDS IN SPECIFIED CIRCUMSTANCES IN 1994

		Predicted Poverty Rate (%)
A	Never-married woman, age 25, living alone, unemployed, social class 5	52.4
B	As A, male	64.8
C	As A, widowed	40.2
D	As A, age 67, and retired	3.0
E	As A, at work for pay	4.1
F	Female lone parent, age 25, one child, home duties, social class 5	80.0
G	As F, male	87.0
H	As F, at work for pay	13.4
I	As F, age 40	69.5
J	As F, age 40 and widowed	58.2

Case F, in the next row of the table, shows the predicted poverty rate for a female lone parent age 25 with one child, engaged in home duties and whose usual occupation would place her in the semi-skilled manual social class (social class 5). The rest of the table shows, for that lone parent case, that the poverty rate would be very much reduced if she was at work for pay, and somewhat lower though still relatively high if she was older.

In summary, the table illustrates a number of points:

- The effect of any given factor (such as economic status of head) depends on the level of risk faced by the household as a result of other factors;

- The risk of poverty is substantially reduced where the household head is in paid employment;

- The poverty risk is lower where the head is retired, than where the head is unemployed or engaged on home duties; and

- When one controls for other factors, female-headed households have a lower risk of poverty than non-couple households headed by males.

Expected Poverty Rate in 1994 if Certain Factors had not Changed

At this stage we turn to an examination of the importance of each of these factors in accounting for the *change in poverty risk* for female-headed households between 1987 and 1994. We use the coefficients from the final model in Table 3.2 to ask what the poverty rate in 1994 for female-headed households would be if factors such as household composition, marital status, and economic status had remained the same as in 1987.

The actual poverty rate for female-headed households in 1987 was nine per cent, and by 1994 this had increased to 25 per cent. The rows in Table 3.3 show the predicted poverty risk if each of the factors identified in the final model were changed one at a time from their 1994 level to their 1987 level. For instance, if the average age of heads in female-headed households remained at 60 rather than falling to the actual 1994 level of 58 (but all other factors remained the same), we would expect the poverty rate in 1994 to be 23.4 per cent. If the proportion of female heads living alone had remained at 51 per cent rather than falling to 48 per cent, we would expect a slightly higher poverty rate (25.4 per cent) in 1994.

The change in the predicted poverty level attributable to each factor is a function of the amount by which the factor changed and the size of the effect of the factor from the final model. Thus, although employment status of the household head was identified as the major factor accounting for differences in poverty risk among non-couple households in 1994, it contributes relatively little to the change in poverty risk for female-headed households between the two time periods because it changed very little.

TABLE 3.3: EXPECTED POVERTY RATE OF FEMALE-HEADED HOUSEHOLDS IN 1994 IF HOUSEHOLD COMPOSITION AND ECONOMIC STATUS OF HOUSEHOLD MEMBERS HAD REMAINED AT 1987 LEVELS.

	Mean		Predicted Poverty if Mean Remained at 1987 Level (%)	Observed Minus Predicted
	1987	*1994*		
Age of head	60.3	58.0	23.4	−1.6
Number of children	0.4	0.6	24.4	−0.6
Number of adults	1.7	1.5	23.7	−1.3
Pre-family household	0.1	0.1	26.0	1.0
Head is widowed	0.6	0.5	23.7	−1.3
Head at work	0.2	0.2	24.8	−0.2
Head retired	0.1	0.2	25.5	0.5
Number of others at work	0.4	0.2	22.0	−3.0
Head is in manual social class	0.5	0.4	25.2	0.2
Living alone	0.5	0.5	25.4	0.4
All variables at 1987 level			19.5	−5.5

We see that the single change which contributed most to the increase in poverty risk for female-headed households was the drop in the number of other adults in the household who were working for pay. Between 1987 and 1994 the average number of other adults in female-headed households who worked for pay dropped from 0.42 to 0.24. If the average had remained at the 1987 level, we would expect a poverty rate in 1994 of 22 per cent, 3 percentage points lower than the rate actually observed.

The final row of Table 3.3 shows the impact on poverty risk if all of the factors had remained at their 1987 levels. If all of the variables in the table remained at their 1987 level, we see that the predicted poverty rate in 1994 would be 19.5 per cent rather than the actual 25 per cent. Overall, then, changes in the profile of female-headed households in terms of age of head, numbers of children, adults and other household members at work, per cent of households at the pre-family stage, whether the head lives alone, is widowed, is at work or retired, or is in a manual social class, account for about one third of the increased risk faced by female-headed households between 1987 and 1994. This means that the remainder of the increase in risk (more than 10 percentage points) cannot be accounted for by changes in the factors which were seen to be the important determinants of poverty risk for these households in 1994.

The bulk of the change between 1987 and 1994, then, is not due to changes in household composition or the economic status of members of female-headed households. In other analyses we explored whether the *effects* of these variables had changed substantially between the two time periods: in other words, were things like earnings less effective in 1994 than in 1987 in protecting from poverty risk? Was there a greater risk associated with the number of children in the household in 1994 than in 1987? It emerged, however, that changes in the impact of these factors on poverty could also account for only a small proportion (about one eighth) of the change.[5] Much of the increased risk for

---

[5] The main changes in effects of variables were absence of an age-of-head effect in 1987; larger impacts of numbers of children and numbers of adults in household; pre-family households were more advantaged; in terms of economic status of the head, there was no gap between those at work and those in home duties, while those who were unemployed had an increased risk and those retired a reduced risk of poverty. Others at work had no effect on poverty risk; head's class had no effect; those living alone were less likely to be poor.

female-headed households between 1987 and 1994 was thus attributable to factors not captured in our models.

A key factor contributing to that observed increase in risk which is not attributable to changes in the profile of the households themselves is in fact straightforward: the trends in the level of social welfare support provided to different types of household over the period. As spelt out in detail elsewhere, (notably Callan *et al*, 1996 and Callan, Nolan and Whelan, 1996), the policy with regard to social welfare rates followed over the 1987–1994 period was to give substantially greater increases to the schemes which, at the start of the period, provided the lowest level of support. This was consistent with the recommendations of the Commission on Social Welfare (1986) that priority be given to bringing up these lowest rates.

As a result, the support paid to an adult on long-term Unemployment Assistance increased by as much as 66 per cent between 1987 and 1994, whereas the old age or widow's pension rate for a single person rose by less than half that figure, as did the support available to lone parents. With average disposable household income rising by about 42 per cent over the period, this meant that the rates of support payable for the schemes on which many female-headed households rely lagged behind average incomes. As a result, by 1994 they were at or about the 50 per cent relative poverty line, whereas in 1987 they had been above that level. This brings out the importance of the relationship between social welfare support levels and average incomes in explaining poverty trends over time, and of the rates paid for certain schemes in particular in influencing poverty risks for female-headed households.

Modelling Risk for Couple-Headed Households

We now use the logit modelling approach to examine the extent to which characteristics of the female partner are important in analysing the poverty risk of what we have called couple households. As noted earlier, couple households are those where a married or cohabiting couple is jointly responsible for the accommodation, or where the responsible person is living with a spouse or partner. There has been a tendency in research on a range of social issues to ignore the characteristics of the female partner and to classify households according to the economic status, social class, age and so on of the husband. This has been justified on the grounds that one can predict important things about households without taking the corresponding characteristics of the female partner into account. In the following section we assess the extent to which this is true of poverty risk.

As in the previous section, our strategy is to run a series of logit models, now for couple households, that examine the impact of a similar set of factors on poverty risk. In doing so we explicitly include characteristics of the male and female partner, such as age, economic status and social class. Table A3.4[6] shows the set of logit models for couple households. The base model (Model 1) shows the coefficient predicting the poverty risk for the average couple household, which corresponds to a poverty risk of 17 per cent. In Model 2, the age of the male partner and the numbers of children and adults in the household are added. Unlike the non-couple households where age was associated with reduced poverty risk in the corresponding model, the age of the male in couple households has no significant association with poverty risk. However, the number of children and the number of adults in the household follow the same pattern as in non-couple households: poverty risk increases as the number of children rises and risk falls as the number of adults rises.

Model 3 adds the life-cycle stage variables, with post-family couple households being the omitted category. All of the life-cycle stages shown have a lower risk of poverty than post-family households. Notice that the coefficient for age of the male partner is now significant and negative. What seems to be happening is that the risk of poverty for couple households is higher at the post-family stage than at other life-cycle stages, but that it drops as the male partner grows older. We will see in later models that it is at retirement age that this drop takes place. This means that, on average and controlling for household composition, post-family households up to retirement age have a higher risk of poverty.

In Model 4, we add three variables for the economic status of the male partner. The comparison group includes cases where he is in education, ill or disabled. Households where the male partner

---

[6] See Appendix, p. 137

is unemployed have a significantly higher risk of poverty, while those where he is working for pay or retired have a significantly lower risk than the comparison group.

In the next model (Model 5) we add the age of the female partner and the three variables measuring her economic status. The comparison group here includes cases where she is engaged in home duties, ill or disabled or in education. Households where the female partner is unemployed do not differ significantly from the comparison group, but as we saw earlier there are actually very few such households in the sample. Where the wife/female partner is working for pay, the poverty risk of households is substantially reduced. The coefficient for where she is retired does not quite reach statistical significance at conventional levels, but the sign is negative, the same direction as the corresponding coefficient for the man. Households where the female partner is older have a reduced risk of poverty; and when that variable is taken into account the male partner's age does not have a statistically significant effect.

In Model 6, the social class of the man is added. As expected, there is an increasing risk of poverty as we move from higher professional and managerial social class (the omitted group) to the unskilled manual social class. The risk is also high where the social class is unknown — typically because he has never worked. The social class of the female partner is introduced in Model 7. When we have controlled for her partner's social class, the social class of the woman does not have a statistically significant impact on poverty risk. An additional model (not shown here) revealed that this remained true even in the case of women working outside the home.

Model 8 adds the measures of the economic status of other household members. The number of other adults (apart from the husband and wife) who are at work is associated with a reduced risk of poverty, as we might expect. The number of other adults unemployed is also associated with a reduced risk of poverty, perhaps reflecting the income they are likely to be receiving from social welfare payments. However, the effect of unemployment among other household members is much smaller than the effect of their participation in paid employment, and proved not to be statistically significant as we dropped other variables to arrive at the final model.

The final model, Model 9, was reached by an iterative process of sequentially dropping non-significant coefficients, and examining changes in the remaining coefficients for patterns which could be captured more parsimoniously by collapsing categories of the variables. For instance, a check on the impact of the female partner's age revealed that it was households where the wife is over age 65 that had the reduced poverty risk. This is plausible in that women in low-income households become entitled to a non-contributory old age pension in their own right on reaching age 66. Also, it emerged as the other social class categories for the female partner were dropped that where the female partner is in the routine non-manual social class, the poverty risk of the household is reduced. This might have to do with the relationship between the class of the partners. If it is the case that women in the two professional and managerial classes almost always have partners in these classes, then membership of these social classes will not have an independently discernible effect. On the other hand, if a substantial proportion of women in routine non-manual occupations have partners in manual occupations, then the two social class measures may be sufficiently independent for them to have distinct effects. This issue deserves further exploration.

The final column in Table A3.4 shows the impact of each factor on the poverty risk of a set of households that would otherwise experience the average poverty rate for all couple households (which was 17 per cent). Again, as noted in the discussion of the models for non-couple households, the actual impact of each factor will depend on whether the risk for a set of households would otherwise be high or relatively low. Where the risk of poverty would otherwise be high, the impact of factors tending to increase poverty risk would be reduced, while the impact of factors tending to reduce poverty risk would be increased. The main purpose of the estimates in the final column is to allow a comparison of the relative importance of the different factors when taken separately.

Among the factors tending to reduce poverty risk, the most important are the economic statuses of the two partners. Where either works the risk of poverty is substantially reduced. The impact of the woman working for pay is roughly of the same magnitude as the man working for pay: each would reduce the poverty risk by about 15 percentage points on average. We know from research on women's pay that women's earnings are likely to be lower than men's, but the earnings of the female partner may still be sufficient to pull the household out of poverty. There may, however, be a selection effect operating here, in that women with higher earning capacity are more likely to be drawn into the paid workforce. This means that if other women who are not working for pay at the moment were to begin working, the impact of their earnings on poverty might not be as great.[7]

Another point to note is that in households where the female partner is age 65 or over the poverty risk is reduced by at least as much as in households where the male partner is retired, while her "retirement" has no significant effect. This suggests that age of the female partner is capturing the income flow associated with entitlement to old age or retirement pensions more accurately than the economic status "retired". We will return in the conclusion to the issue of the different meaning attached by men and women to the economic status categories.

Other factors tending to reduce poverty risk are, in order of size of the effect, the presence of one other adult at work, and the life-cycle stage where there are grown children still living in the household. In addition, households where the youngest child is under age four have a slightly lower risk of poverty than we would otherwise expect based on household composition and the labour force status of household members. Each additional child in the household adds a small amount to the household's poverty risk.

Of the factors tending to increase poverty risk, male partner's social class has the largest effect. The female partner's social class then has little effect. This may reflect the fact that differences between the classes of the partners were limited, or that the social class categories are less useful in capturing the variations in life-chances associated with the kinds of jobs in which most women

---

[7] There is some evidence of this if we compare the impact of the wife working for pay in 1987 and 1994: the coefficient for wife's work in 1987 was higher. In 1987, there were fewer wives working for pay. Those wives who were in the paid labour force were probably an even more select group than they were in 1994, with higher expected earnings than wives in general.

work or their pattern of labour force participation throughout the life-cycle.

Table 3.5 provides an alternative view of the results of the logit model by looking at the predicted poverty rate for couple households in specified circumstances. The "baseline" household in the first row of the table consists of a couple with two children, where the woman is aged 35, the youngest child is under age five, the man is working for pay and the woman is engaged on home duties and not working for pay. The model predicts a poverty rate of 11.3 per cent for households in this situation. If the woman were instead working for pay, the poverty risk would be virtually eliminated. If the male partner in the baseline household was unemployed (and the woman was engaged on home duties) the poverty risk would rise dramatically to about 60 per cent. However, with the male unemployed if the wife were to begin working in paid employment the risk of poverty would again be reduced to 15 per cent, only slightly above the rate for households where only the male partner works for pay.

TABLE 3.5: PREDICTED POVERTY RATE FOR COUPLE HOUSEHOLDS IN SPECIFIED CIRCUMSTANCES, 1994

	Type of Case	Predicted Poverty Rate (%)
A	Couple, woman age 35; 2 children, youngest under 5; man works for pay; woman engaged in home duties, not working for pay	11.3
B	As A, + woman works for pay	1.5
C	As A, + man unemployed	59.9
D	As A, + man unemployed, woman works for pay	15.0
E	As A, 5 children aged from 3 to 15	30.0
F	Young couple, no children; man works for pay; woman works at home	7.7
G	Elderly couple, both retired; Social Class 4, 3; live with one daughter age 25, who works for pay.	0.6
H	As G, daughter moves out	5.7
	All couple households	16.8

If there were five children instead of two in the baseline household, the poverty risk would increase from 11 to 30 per cent, while a household similar to the baseline case in all respects but with no children would have a poverty risk of about eight per cent. This again illustrates the point that the lower the expected poverty rate, the less the impact of factors which tend to reduce poverty, and the greater the impact of factors which tend to increase poverty risk.

Case "G" is a household consisting of an elderly couple, where both partners are retired. The male partner's former job placed him in the skilled manual social class while the female partner formerly worked in a routine non-manual occupation, and an adult daughter who is working for pay lives with the couple. The poverty risk for households in this situation is less than 1 per cent. If the daughter moves out, the poverty risk increases markedly to almost six per cent, but remains well below the average for all couple households.

A final statistic which we might use in order to assess the importance of women's paid work in keeping households out of poverty is to ask what the poverty rate for couple households would be if none of the female partners worked for pay. As with the figures in Table A3.4 we make the estimation assuming that all of the other characteristics of households remain at their present level. The first column (where the mean of the independent variables are shown) shows that the female partner works for pay in 30 per cent of couple households. If this was reduced to 0 while all other factors remained the same, the estimates suggest that the poverty rate of couple households would be 28 per cent rather than the actual rate of 17 per cent. This would bring the poverty rate of couple households close to the 32 per cent faced by female lone parent households in 1994.

Conclusions and Implications

In this chapter we looked first at the position of female-headed households (i.e., households where the person responsible for the accommodation was a single, widowed, divorced or separated woman rather than a man or a couple). We found that in 1994, household composition and the economic status of household members were critical determinants of poverty risk. Indeed, when these factors are fully taken into account, female-headed households would otherwise have had a slightly lower risk of poverty than households headed by a single, widowed, divorced or separated man.

Changes in these characteristics accounted for some of the sharp increase in the risk of poverty for female-headed households between 1987 and 1994. The important contributory factors were the reduction in the number of adults, particularly those working for pay, in these households, and the increase in the proportion of female heads who were younger, never-married or separated and with children under age 18, rather than older, widowed with no dependent children. However, these changes in the profile of female-headed households still only accounted for about one third of the increase in risk experienced by this group between 1987 and 1994.

The key factor accounting for much of the remaining increase in risk is in fact straightforward: the trends in the level of social welfare support provided to different types of household over the period. Consistent with the recommendations of the Commission on Social Welfare (1986), over the 1987–1994 period substantially greater increases were given for the schemes which, at the start of the period, provided the lowest level of support. As a result, the support paid to an adult on long-term unemployment assistance increased by as much as 66 per cent between 1987 and 1994, whereas the old age or widow's pension rate for a single person rose by less than half that figure, as did the support available to lone parents. With average disposable household income rising by about 42 per cent over the period, this meant that by 1994 the rates of support payable for the schemes on which many female-headed households rely were at or about the 50 per cent relative poverty line, whereas in 1987 they had been above that level. This brings out the importance of the relationship between social welfare support levels and average incomes in explaining poverty trends over time, and of the rates paid for certain schemes in particular in influencing poverty risks for female-headed households. It is worth noting in this context that since 1994 old age pensions have risen faster than unemployment payments, and that an explicit commitment has been given that the contributory old age pension will reach £100 per week by the year 2002.

As far as households headed by a couple are concerned, the results showed the main determinants of poverty risk to be the economic status of both partners and of others in the household, social class of the male partner, and household composition (number of children and number of adults). Women's paid work was seen to reduce poverty by about the same amount as men's paid work. The female partner being aged over 65 and the male partner being retired were found to have similar effects. Additional children in the household increased poverty risk, while the presence of additional adults slightly reduced it, even if these adults were not working for pay

The interpretation one places upon these findings and their implications depend crucially on the kind of causal ordering we see as applying to the different factors. It also has implications for the most satisfactory classifications of households to employ in analysing poverty risk. For instance, we have seen that households with grown children have a substantially reduced risk of poverty. The logit analysis revealed that this was mainly because these households were likely to have more adults at work. Does this mean that we should abandon the classification of households in terms of life-cycle stage, and instead use a classification system based simply on the numbers of children and adults in the household? One reason why we might not want to adopt this approach is that the life-cycle stage classification system summarises a number of interrelated factors: presence of children, presence of other adults and probable economic status of these adults.

Of more direct relevance to this study is whether we abandon the concept of "female-headed households", because much of the contrast between households headed by women and those headed by men is captured by factors such as household composition and the economic status of household members. A strong argument for retaining the concept is related to the causal assumptions that underlie much feminist analysis. If we believe that broader causal factors are operating to disadvantage women both in terms of their greater, uncompensated responsibility for children and in terms of their situation in the labour market, then the gender of the household head is causally prior to factors such as household composition and economic status. In other words, female-headed households are poorer because they are likely to contain fewer adults and more children, and because the head is less likely to be working for pay. But the fact that these households contain fewer adults and more children and the head is less likely to be working for pay are themselves related to the fact that the head is a woman and the broader socio-economic status of women. The concept of the female-headed household may thus be a crucial one from the perspective of concerns with equality more generally.

An important caveat is in order, however. The meaning of "female-headed" household and "male-headed" households needs to be clearly defined. In much of the existing research on poverty and disadvantage "male-headed" households are defined to include couple households. This leads to a number of conceptual problems. First, when comparing "male-headed" households thus defined to female-headed households we are not comparing like with like, since couple households have at least two adults, whereas many female-headed households comprise single women living alone or a woman living with dependent children. The comparison thus runs the risk of confounding household composition effects with the effects of disadvantage experienced by women because of their general socio-economic position.

A second danger is that in focusing on the sex of the household head, we will lose sight of the fact that most adult women live in couple households. This could have the effect of overlooking the important contribution that their paid work makes to keeping couple households out of poverty. These are issues to which we return in the next chapter.

Chapter 4

THE POVERTY RISK OF INDIVIDUALS AND CATEGORISING HOUSEHOLDS

Introduction

As we have argued in the previous chapter, focusing exclusively on female-headed households is problematic. It can confound the impact on poverty risk of living arrangements with those of gender-differentiated life-chances, and miss the situation of women in households headed by a couple. In order to explore in more depth the significance of changes in living arrangements between 1987 and 1994, we shift the focus in the first part of this chapter from households to individuals. In other words, we take the individual rather than the household as the unit of analysis, and examine the risk faced by women versus men of being in a poor household.

In doing so, we retain the assumption that living standards are equalised within the household due to sharing of resources: the issue of possible differences in poverty risks between individuals within the household is considered in Chapter 6. We examine the way in which the poverty risk of individual adult men and women changed between 1987 and 1994, still basing the identification of those who are poor/non-poor on the (equivalised) income of the household of which they are members. We pay particular attention to young unattached adults and to lone parents, since it is the increased poverty risk among women living alone and among lone parents that is driving the increased risk faced by female-headed households between 1987 and 1994.

In the second part of the chapter we bring together these findings with those of Chapters 2 and 3 on poverty risk for households. We use them to inform a discussion of how best to develop a system of classifying households that goes beyond characteristics of the household head and captures the main factors responsible for household level variation in poverty risk.

The Poverty Risk of Individuals

The definition of poverty we employ continues to be based on the total income of the household, but we are now exploring the risk faced by adult men and women of being in a household whose total income is below relative income poverty lines. It is useful to begin with an overview of the poverty risk of all adult men and women in 1987 and 1994. Table 4.1 compares the situation of all men and women at these two points in time, using three different relative income lines.

TABLE 4.1: RISKS OF POVERTY FOR MEN AND WOMEN IN 1987 AND 1994

	1987 — Per cent below Poverty Line		
	Male	*Female*	*Total*
40% line	6.4	5.5	5.9
50% line	16.0	14.6	15.3
60% line	25.5	25.7	25.6
Total in population	1,112,482	1,131,483	2,243,965
	1994 — Per cent below Poverty Line		
	Male	*Female*	*Total*
40% line	5.3	5.7	5.5
50% line	15.5	18.1	16.8
60% line	28.1	33.0	30.6
Total in population	1,266,777	1,313,622	2,580,399

In 1987 men and women faced very similar risks of being in a poor household, at all three income poverty line cut-offs. If anything, men had a marginally higher risk of being in households below the 50 per cent income line. By 1994, a gap had begun to emerge in the opposite direction, particularly at the 50 per cent and 60 per cent poverty lines, with the magnitude of the difference increasing as we move from the 50 per cent to the 60 per cent poverty line. The fact that the poverty gender gap for individuals is much less than for female-headed versus other household types reflects the fact that, as we shall see in the next table, most adult women live in couple households.

We have already seen in Chapter 2 that between 1987 and 1994 there was an increase in the proportion of individuals living alone, a decline in the proportion of households consisting of couples and children, and a decline in the number of adults in couple and children households. All of these trends suggest that young adults may be likely to set up a household in their own right at an earlier stage. Our analysis at this stage is designed to explore the impact on the poverty risk of individuals of different kinds of living arrangements.

Living arrangements, as understood here, refer mainly to whether the individual is a household head (or partner) in their own right, or is living as a member of a household in which some-one else is the head. In the majority of cases, younger household members who are not heads are the grown-up children of the household head. In such situations, the individual will be living in a "couple and children" household if both parents are present, or in a "lone parent" household if only one parent is present. In the context of the overall focus on women and poverty, we are particularly concerned to establish whether young adult women who are single or are lone parents are at a higher risk of poverty if they become household heads than if they lived in the family home.

In subsequent tables, we further distinguish between adults in four different situations:

- "Unattached" adults — those who are not living in a marital or cohabiting relationship and either have no children or whose children are grown and have left home. This group is further divided into two groups based on the broad life-cycle stage categories used earlier: those under 45 and those aged 45 and over.

- Lone parents — those with children (of any age) still living in the household and not living in a marital or cohabiting relationship. This group is also subdivided into those aged under 45 and those aged 45 or over.

- Married/cohabiting individuals — those living in a marital or cohabiting relationship with or without children living in the household.

Table 4.2 and Table 4.3 show the living arrangements of male and female individuals in each of these categories in 1987 and 1994, respectively.

We see that in 1987, 62 per cent of men and 61 per cent of women lived in couple households in which they were the joint heads. This had fallen to 55 per cent of men and 52 per cent of women by 1994, mainly because of an increase in the proportion who were "unattached" and under 45. The proportion of all adult women who were lone parents under the age of 45 had also increased in this period, from two per cent in 1987 to six per cent in 1994.

Most younger unattached individuals, both male and female, live in households in which they are not the household head. This is usually a couple and children household, and less frequently a lone parent household. Younger unattached women are slightly less likely than their male counterparts to be household heads. This reflects the fact that women tend to marry a few years earlier than men and move to joint headship of couple households. For both men and women the proportion of younger unattached individuals who are household heads increased slightly between 1987 and 1994.

By contrast, most lone parents and older unattached individuals are household heads. The proportion of older unattached individuals who were household heads had increased for both males and females between 1987 and 1994. Virtually all married or cohabiting couples have set up a household in their own right rather than living with their parents as non-heads of households.

To what extent are young lone parents or young unattached individuals at a reduced risk of poverty if they continue to live in the family home rather than setting up households in their own right? Table 4.4 shows how the risk of poverty is affected by the living arrangements of adult individuals. Generally speaking, those who are household heads face a greater risk of poverty than similarly attached individuals who are not household heads.

TABLE 4.2: PER CENT OF ALL ADULT MEN AND ALL ADULT WOMEN IN EACH ATTACHMENT STATUS, AND LIVING ARRANGEMENT IN 1987

	Attachment Status					
	Unattached, under 45	Unattached, over 45	Lone parent, under 45	Lone parent, over 45	Married/ Cohabiting	Total
Male						
Household head	3.0	6.6	0.1	1.5	62.5	73.7
With couple & children	15.9	0.5	–	0.1	0.5	17.0
With lone parent	5.2	0.7	–	0	0.3	6.2
With other	1.0	1.2	–	0.3	0.6	3.1
Total	25.2	9.1	0.1	1.9	63.8	100.0
Female						
Household head	1.4	8.5	1.7	5.0	61.4	78.0
With couple & children	11.1	0.7	0.5	0.6	0.4	13.3
With lone parent	3.0	0.2	0.1	0.2	0.2	3.7
With other	1.8	1.8	0.1	0.8	0.5	5.0
Total	17.3	11.2	2.4	6.5	62.6	100.0

TABLE 4.3: PER CENT OF ALL ADULT MEN AND ALL ADULT WOMEN IN EACH ATTACHMENT STATUS, AND LIVING ARRANGEMENT IN 1994

	Attachment Status					
	Unattached, under 45	Unattached, over 45	Lone parent, under 45	Lone parent, over 45	Married/ cohabiting	Total
Male						
Household head	4.6	8.2	0.2	1.2	54.8	68.9
With couple & children	21.4	0.2	0	0.1	0.1	21.9
With lone parent	5.9	0.5		0.1	0.4	6.9
With other	1.1	0.9		0.0	0.2	2.2
Total	33.1	9.8	0.2	1.4	55.5	100.0
Female						
Household head	2.5	9.9	3.7	4.6	52.5	73.2
With couple & children	15.8	0.3	1.3	0.8	0.1	18.3
With lone parent	3.4	0.3	0.5	0.1	0.4	4.6
With other	1.4	1.6	0.1	0.6	0.2	3.9
Total	23.1	12.1	5.5	6.1	53.2	100.0

This probably reflects the overall lower risk of poverty experienced by households with a larger number of adults. An exception to this general pattern is found for younger unattached individuals, where the risk of poverty tends to be greater when they are living as non-heads, usually in the family home. This suggests that young unattached individuals tend to defer setting up a household in their own right until they can afford to do so without facing poverty. However, the extent to which this is true declined between 1987 and 1994: the poverty rate for both male and female young unattached household heads had increased over this period.

In both years, the poverty risk for young unattached male heads was greater than for their female counterparts. However, the reverse is true for non-heads: by 1994 the risk of poverty was considerably higher for young unattached women who were not household heads than for their male counterparts, particularly in a lone parent household. It does not appear, then, that remaining in the family home would have the effect of "protecting" young adults from poverty overall. However, when one controls for the economic status of the individual (whether at work, unemployed etc.), this picture may change, as we explore shortly.

There is some indication that, particularly by 1994, lone mothers who continue to live in the family home rather than moving out to form an independent household in their own right experience a reduced risk of being in a poor household. For lone mothers, the poverty rate was 11 per cent if living with both her own parents and six per cent if living with one parent (usually a widowed mother), compared with 32 per cent for lone parents who are household heads in their own right. About 18 per cent of female lone parents live in a household headed by a couple with children. Later we will check whether this pattern still holds when one controls for the labour force status of the individual.

TABLE 4.4: POVERTY RISK BY LIVING ARRANGEMENTS, LIFE-CYCLE STAGE AND SEX, 1987 AND 1994

	Unattached, under 45	Lone Parent	Unattached, 45 or over	Married/ Cohabiting
	Per cent poor			
Male 1987				
Household head	6.8	16.6	26.4	17.6
Not head/partner, lives with ...				
Couple & children	11.2	0	7.1	3.6
Lone parent	9.8	0	19.3	11.6
Other	0.0	0	13.0	16.3
Female 1987				
Household head	0.0	16.6	4.4	17.6
Not head/partner, lives with ...				
Couple & children	10.7	10.4	25.2	3.6
Lone parent	4.7	12.8	5.5	11.6
Other	1.5	12.2	18.1	16.3

	Unattached, under 45	Lone Parent	Unattached, 45 or over	Married/ Cohabiting
	Per cent poor			
Male 1994				
Household head	12.2	11.9	21.1	17.0
Not head/partner, lives with ...				
Couple & children	12.2	0.0	6.0	0.0
Lone parent	15.7	0.0	0.0	4.6
Other	1.2	0.0	11.5	0.0
Female 1994				
Household head	9.8	32.7	22.5	17.1
Not head/partner, lives with ...				
Couple & children	16.5	10.6	20.4	0.0
Lone parent	23.5	5.9	15.1	4.0
Other	3.6	1.7	3.5	0.0

Young Unattached Individuals

Table 4.5 shows the poverty risk for young unattached individuals categorised by their living arrangements and whether they are working for pay. We saw earlier that households headed by un-employed males or by females engaged in home duties were at an increased risk of poverty (62 per cent and 37 per cent, respectively in 1994). The figures here illustrate the way in which living arrangements can "insulate" adult individuals from some of the effects of not earning. In 1994, the poverty rate for men who were not earning was 44 per cent if they were the household head, but dropped below 24 per cent if they were not the household head. The pattern was very similar in 1987, but with a higher poverty rate for household heads.

TABLE 4.5: POVERTY RISK OF YOUNG (UNDER 45) UNATTACHED ADULTS BY ECONOMIC STATUS AND LIVING ARRANGEMENTS IN 1987 AND 1994 (%)

	1987		1994	
	Working for Pay	*Other Economic Status*	*Working for Pay*	*Other Economic Status*
Male				
Household head	2.6	51.0	1.6	43.6
With couple & children	3.3	21.9	3.7	20.1
With lone parent	4.1	16.0	6.0	23.8
With other	0.0	0.0	0.0	3.4
Female				
Household head	0.0	0.0	0.0	64.2
With couple & children	5.2	26.3	3.8	27.0
With lone parent	2.9	10.4	5.3	33.4
With other	0.0	39.1	0.0	17.7

The "insulating" effect of living arrangements for younger unat-tached women is also apparent. In 1994, 64 per cent of this group who were not earning and who were household heads were poor, compared to less than one third of women in the same economic situation who were not household heads. Being the household head exposes the individual to the risk of poverty associated with labour force status to a greater extent than occupying some other position in the household. The pattern was somewhat different for women in 1987, in that young unattached women who headed households had an extremely low poverty risk.

The other major point to be drawn from the table is the very low risk of poverty faced by young men and women who are at work for pay. The figures indicate clearly that for younger unattached men and women, and irrespective of whether they are household heads or living with their families, the poverty risk is very low where the individual is working for pay.

Younger (under 45) Lone Mothers

Table 4.6 shows the poverty risk of lone mothers under age 45 by their own economic status and living arrangements in 1987 and 1994. In 1987, the poverty risk for a younger lone mother who was a household head was reduced to about half (17 per cent compared to 39 per cent) if she worked for pay. The insulating effect of living as a member of a larger household is also evident for this group, particularly if the lone mother lived with both her parents (the couple and children household type).

By 1994, the importance of the lone mother's own earnings in reducing poverty risk had increased dramatically. If a lone mother who was a household head did not earn, her risk of poverty had increased from 39 per cent in 1987 to 67 per cent in 1994. If she worked, however, her risk of poverty in 1994 had dropped to three per cent (compared to 17 per cent in 1987). In 1994, the insulating effect of living in a larger household is still apparent for younger lone mothers, but only where they do not earn. The poverty risk for younger lone mothers who earn is actually higher if she lives in a household headed by a couple and children. However, the decrease in risk for those not earning who live in larger households is very marked indeed.

TABLE 4.6: POVERTY RISK OF YOUNGER (UNDER 45) LONE MOTHERS BY LIVING ARRANGEMENTS, ECONOMIC STATUS AND SEX, 1987 AND 1994*

	Per cent in Poverty			
	1987		**1994**	
	Working for Pay	*Other Economic Status*	*Working for Pay*	*Other Economic Status*
Household head	16.9	38.7	2.5	66.7
With couple and children	7.3	12.5	5.4	17.5
With lone parent	----*	30.7	30.4	2.7
With other	----*	----*	----*	----*

* Broken lines (----) indicate that there were too few cases in the sample to provide a reliable estimate.

Alternatives to Household Head as way of Classifying Households

The analysis up to this point clearly points to the need to go beyond simply the characteristics of the household head in attempting to understand the way poverty risk varies across households. In particular, as well as considering household composition, the economic status of other household members (especially the spouse or partner in couple households) needs to be taken into account. In this section we draw on the range of results we have presented so far to discuss the implications for how best to categorise households in analysing poverty, and in particular poverty among women.

In couple households, the head is traditionally defined as the male partner. Our analysis of couple households clearly suggests that even when one controls for characteristics of the male partner (age, whether unemployed, whether at work, social class), poverty risk is significantly reduced if the wife works for pay. The magnitude of the effect of the wife's work is on a par with the magnitude of the effect of the husband's work, suggesting that women's work is particularly important at the margin in keeping households out of poverty.

Any classification scheme for households in poverty analysis would certainly need to take account of the number of adults and the number of children in the household. One-person households and households with dependent children, particularly lone-parent households, emerged from our results as at higher risk of poverty in 1994. The life-cycle stage of the household is also important as we have seen. Pre-family households and households with "grown children" are at a relatively low risk of poverty; while the risk is higher where there are young children in the household. In addition, there is a tendency for poverty risk to drop as the household head (or joint heads in a couple household) reach retirement. We have also seen that whether the wife is at work in a couple household has an impact on the poverty risk of the household as a whole, even when the husband's labour force status is taken into account. In addition, a household with other members working for pay also faced a reduced risk of poverty.

The problem one faces in seeking to take account of such a range of factors is that a classification system must also be tractable. Suppose, for example, that one starts with a labour force status measure with ten categories: for any individual in the household this is entirely manageable. Suppose though that we try to capture the labour force status of both partners in a couple: we now have one hundred possible combinations (many with only very small numbers in them). Nor is there any reason to believe that one particular way of categorising households will be best for all purposes. Depending on the objective of the analysis, different ways of looking at the data will be more satisfactory. However, it is worth illustrating some possible approaches to the problem which go beyond the characteristics of the "household head".

One approach is to continue to focus on the characteristics of one individual in the household, but redefine the basis on which that individual is selected. Most obviously, one can measure directly who is currently contributing most to the income of the household, and concentrate on that individual as what the Central Statistics Office, for example, term the principal economic supporter. An alternative which has been developed by sociologists in the context of classification by social class is called the dominance approach (see Erikson, 1984; Breen and Whelan, 1996). This involves classifying all married persons according to the class position of whichever partner is considered "dominant", where two criteria of dominance apply. The first is that employment dominates non-employment and full-time employment dominates part-time employment. The second is that higher level employment in terms of position in a class schema dominates lower level employment.

Without going into the precise details of how this is done in practice, it is worth applying this approach to selecting the "dominant" partner in couple households in our 1994 sample, and illustrating the extent to which this affects key results in terms of poverty. Table 4.7 first shows the poverty rate (still using the 50 per cent poverty line) for households in that sample categorised by the labour force status of the household head or, in the case of couple households, the male partner. It then shows the corresponding results when the labour force status of the "dominant" partner, in the sense just outlined, is used instead to categorise households. We see that there is very little difference between the two, reflecting the fact that the dominance approach does not in fact lead to recategorisation of many households in terms of labour force status.[1]

TABLE 4.7: POVERTY RATE FOR HOUSEHOLDS CATEGORISED BY LABOUR FORCE STATUS OF "HOUSEHOLD HEAD" VERSUS "DOMINANT PARTNER", 1994

Labour Force Status	"Household Head"	"Dominant Partner"
	Per cent in Poverty	
Employee	6.6	8.7
Self-employed	6.9	6.9
Farmer	8.7	8.7
Unemployed	32.0	29.9
Ill/disabled	8.6	8.6
Retired	10.2	10.2
In home duties	27.1	27.1

---

[1] We are very grateful to our colleague Chris Whelan for providing these results from the dominance approach.

Concentrating on the characteristics of one individual is in any case going to provide only limited information about the household, and may miss features which are particularly important for some types of household no matter which individual is selected. It is thus worth exploring alternative approaches to categorising households which seek to capture more about, for example, the labour force status of both partners in couple households. Drawing on Davies and Joshi (1998), Table 4.8, for example, shows a classification system which incorporates more of the factors which were identified earlier as relevant to the poverty risk of households, whilst keeping to a manageable number of categories.[2] Households are divided into three broad groups based on the age and attachment status of the household head or joint heads:

- Non-elderly couple households: These are households where the head is married or cohabiting, and neither partner is aged 65 or older. These households are further subdivided on the basis of whether neither, one or both partners earn (as employees or as self-employed or farmer), and on the basis of the number of children under 18 in the household (none, one to two, three or more). Since the proportion of households where the wife earns but the husband does not earn is relatively small, these are not subdivided on the basis of the number of children under 18.

- Other non-elderly households: These are divided into lone parent households (where the lone parent has at least one child under 18) and households where the head is "unattached" (no spouse or partner and no dependent children). These households are further subdivided on the basis of whether there is someone in the household who is earning.

- Elderly households: the head (or spouse if it is a couple household) is aged 65 or over. These are further subdivided on the basis of whether someone in the household (not necessarily the household head) is earning.

---

[2] Note that Davies and Joshi base their categories on families rather than households.

We now illustrate the usefulness of such a classification by using it to examine changes in the composition of the population between 1987 and 1994 and changes in poverty risk.

TABLE 4.8: HOUSEHOLD TYPE AND POVERTY RISK IN 1987 AND 1994

	1987		1994	
	% Poor	% of All Households	% Poor	% of All Households
Non-Elderly Couple Households				
Both earning, no children	0.0	3.7	1.1	4.7
Both earning 1–2 children	1.4	4.1	2.5	7.6
Both earning, 3+ children	6.4	2.3	1.2	3.0
Husband only earns, no children	9.8	6.1	4.4	4.8
Husband only earns, 1–2 children	8.4	15.2	9.6	11.5
Husband only earns, 3+ children	15.5	12.7	21.3	8.3
Wife only earns	8.3	2.4	19.0	2.4
Neither earns	56.3	12.0	55.8	10.2
Other Non-Elderly Households				
Lone parent, 1+ earning	10.2	3.5	8.9	3.6
Lone parent, nobody earning	36.8	2.5	60.2	4.7
Unattached, 1+ earning	11.1	7.8	2.6	9.4
Unattached, nobody earning	34.3	3.7	62.0	4.8
Elderly Households				
Elderly, 1+ earner	11.9	8.0	6.7	6.3
Elderly, no earner	5.6	15.8	13.3	18.8
All	16.3	100.0	18.8	100.0

Table 4.8 shows first that the main changes in the profile of the two ESRI samples between 1987 and 1994 were a drop in the overall proportion of non-elderly couple households, a rise in the proportion of other non-elderly households, and a small increase in the proportion of elderly households. There were also important

changes associated with the increase over the period in the proportion of married women at work for pay. The proportion of
households where both partners worked for pay increased from 10
to 15 per cent of all households, while the proportion where only
the husband worked fell from 34 to 25 per cent. Households where
only the wife worked remained relatively stable at only two per
cent of all households, while the proportion of households where
neither partner worked fell slightly from 12 to 10 per cent. By
1994, the wife was working for pay in roughly one third of all couple households.

The figures in the table then show clearly the importance of the
wife's earnings in keeping households out of poverty. The poverty
risk for households where both partners work is very low in both
years, and in 1994 there was no tendency for the very low risk of
poverty in these households to increase with the number of children. In contrast, the risk of poverty for households where only
the husband works is higher and increases sharply as the number
of children in the household increases. In 1987, the risk of poverty
for households where only the wife earns was comparable
(at about eight per cent) to the risk for households with two or
fewer children where only the husband earns. By 1994, however,
the risk has more than doubled for households where only the
wife earns: from eight to 19 per cent — bringing the level close to
that of households with three or more children where only the
husband earns. This suggests that, particularly by 1994, the level
of women's earnings are less adequate than men's in keeping a
household that relies on a single income source out of poverty.

In general, earnings have become more important in keeping
non-couple households out of poverty. Between 1987 and 1994 the
poverty gap between households where someone earns and those
where nobody earns has increased. The poverty risk has fallen for
the other non-elderly households where at least one person works
for pay, but has increased sharply for households where no-one
earns. In 1987 elderly households with no earner had a lower risk
of poverty than those with at least one earner, but this had reversed by 1994. The overall level of poverty for elderly households
in 1994 is not high, however, being on a par with the rate for
couple households with children where only the husband works.

This classification system thus allows one to assess the impact of having at least one earner in the household, the importance of differing numbers of children for couple households, and the importance of women's earnings in couple households. Of the characteristics it does not incorporate, perhaps the most important is the number of earners other than the household head or couple. It does however capture the main elements of household composition, life-cycle stage and the economic status of household members that account for variations in poverty risk.

Many alternative categorisations aiming at the same general objective could be adopted. For example, Table 4.9 shows a slightly more parsimonious classification schema with 11 categories, which does not distinguish elderly versus non-elderly, and has also been used elsewhere. The choice of a particular schema will depend on the precise purpose of the analysis at hand, and that will determine whether for example one wants to incorporate labour force status of other household members at the cost of dropping aspects of household composition such as number of children. The general conclusion we would emphasise at this point, however, is that it is valuable to move beyond categorisations of, for example, labour force status based simply on the characteristics of one individual in the household, and that this can be done in a way that still provides tractable categorisations.

TABLE 4.9: ALTERNATIVE CATEGORISATION BY HOUSEHOLD TYPE

Household Type
Single Persons
Single Parents
Couple, No Children, No Earner
Couple, No Children, 1 Earner
Couple, No Children, 2 Earners
Couple, Children, No Earner
Couple, Children, 1 Earner
Couple, Children, 2 Earners
Singles with Relatives
Couples with Relatives
Other

Summary and Conclusions

This chapter began with a shift in focus from the household to the individual as the unit of analysis. This involved looking at the poverty risk for individual women and men rather than households headed by females versus males or couples, while retaining for the present the assumption that each member of a given household has the same living standard. An overview of the risks of poverty faced by adult men and women in 1987 and 1994 was provided. This showed that the gender gap in poverty risk at the individual level is much smaller than the gap between male-headed, female-headed and couple households. This is because the majority of adult men and women live in couple households, and so face similar risks of being in a poor household. It also showed that there was some increase in the poverty risk faced by adult women compared to that faced by adult men between 1987 and 1994, this being most apparent at the 60 per cent poverty line. About one third of all women, compared with 28 per cent of all men were in households below that line in 1994.

We then turned to a closer examination of the way in which the poverty risk of two groups, namely young unattached individuals and young lone mothers, were affected by their economic status and living arrangements. These two groups are particularly relevant here because it is the gender gap among those living alone and among lone parents that is driving the increased risk of poverty we observed for female-headed households between 1987 and 1994. The results showed that living in a larger household — for example continuing to live in the family home rather than setting up a household in their own right — can insulate young unattached adults and young lone mothers from the poverty risk associated with not earning an income. By 1994, however, where a lone mother works for pay, living in a larger household did not further reduce poverty risk.

These results clearly pointed to the "insulating" effect of sharing accommodation where the individual or lone parent is not earning. Before policy implications are drawn, however, we would need to know more about the potential disadvantages of having a larger number of people sharing accommodation. This is particularly true in the context of the general trend towards smaller household sizes, which would seem to be indicative of a preference for the autonomy associated with establishing a home of one's own. The measure of poverty used here does not take account of the potential disadvantages of sharing accommodation. Apart from the autonomy implications, households with a larger number of adults may be more likely to live in overcrowded conditions.

We then went on to consider how the categorisation of households for the purpose of poverty analysis might go beyond the position of the "household head" to incorporate more of the factors which were identified as relevant to poverty risk of households. One classification system was illustrated, which allowed us to assess the positive impact of having at least one earner in the household, the importance of the presence of differing numbers of children for couple households, and the importance of women's earnings in couple households. A wide range of alternatives could be adopted, with the choice depending on the precise objective of the analysis in question. However, it is clearly both valuable and possible to employ categorisations of, for example, labour force status which are not based on the situation of only one individual in the household but remain tractable.

Chapter 5

WOMEN'S EMPLOYMENT, LOW PAY AND HOUSEHOLD POVERTY

Introduction

Participation by women in the paid labour force has been increasing particularly rapidly in Ireland in recent years, but women are much more likely than men to be working for low levels of pay. In this chapter we first briefly outline overall trends in women's participation in the paid labour force and then focus on the position of women who are working as employees. We analyse the extent to which women's earnings fall below commonly used low pay benchmarks. We look at how many of the women who are low paid also live in poor households, and the contribution which low-paid women's earnings make to keeping households out of poverty. We then examine the impact of unemployment versus employment on psychological distress levels for men versus women. Finally, we examine policy issues around the obstacles facing women who want to take up paid employment.

Our focus here continues to be on women and poverty, rather than on, for example, the differential between male and female earnings throughout the distribution, which can also be studied using the survey data employed here (see Callan and Wren, 1994). That data is once again from the 1987 and 1994 ESRI household surveys, which have been described briefly in Chapter 1 and in more depth in Callan *et al* (1989, 1996).

Women and Employment

The overall rate of participation by Irish women in the paid labour force was stable between 1960 and the early 1980s, while the participation rate of married women was rising slowly. More recently, both the overall participation rate and more particularly that for married women has been rising rapidly. Table 5.1 shows female participation rates in both 1987 and 1994 for Ireland and most other OECD countries. In 1987 the female labour force participation in Ireland was 38 per cent, while many of the other developed countries had female participation rates of over 50 per cent and only Spain had a lower rate than Ireland. By 1994 the participation rate in Ireland had increased to 47 per cent. Very few of the OECD countries for which data are available experienced larger increases.

The increase in the number of Irish women in the paid labour force between 1991 and 1997 exceeded the combined employment increases over the previous 20 years. While there has been a significant increase in the numbers of women in self-employment — more rapid than for men — the bulk of the increase in numbers at work represents employees. However, particularly for women the share of part-time workers among employees has also risen rapidly, from around 11 per cent in the mid-1980s to over 20 per cent. Almost half these part-time women are employed in service occupations, with clerical and professional and technical occupations accounting for most of the remainder.

Focusing now on women at work as employees, household survey data allows the relationship between participation and the position of other household members to be analysed. Callan and Wren (1994) have carried out such an analysis with the ESRI survey for 1987, and a similar exercise based on data from the 1994 survey is currently under way. It is worth noting that the ESRI surveys show the percentage of married women working as employees increasing from 22 per cent in 1987 to 34 per cent in 1994. This is reflected in a rise in the share of gross household income accounted for by female earnings, from 12 per cent in 1987 to 15 per cent in 1994. The impact such changes have had on household inequality are among the issues being addressed in a forthcoming study for the Combat Poverty Agency by Callan,

Nolan, O'Neill and Sweetman (forthcoming 1999). Here we can simply note from Table 5.2 that the increase in employment rates for married women over the period varied considerably depending on the position of the husband in the male earnings distribution — or whether he was employed in the first place.

TABLE 5.1: FEMALE LABOUR FORCE PARTICIPATION RATES (AGE 15–64) IN IRELAND AND OTHER OECD COUNTRIES, 1987 AND 1994

Country	Female Participation Rate 1987 (%)	Female Participation Rate 1994 (%)	Proportional Change in Participation Rate
Australia	56.7	63.4	+12%
Austria	53.0	62.1	+17%
Belgium	49.9	55.1	+10%
Canada	65.5	67.8	+4%
Denmark	76.8	73.8	–4%
Finland	72.9	69.9	–4%
France	55.5	59.6	+7%
Germany	54.5	61.8	+13%
Greece	41.7	44.6	+7%
Ireland	38.5	47.2	+23%
Italy	43.4	42.9	–1%
Japan	57.8	62.1	+7%
Luxembourg	45.7	56.5	+24%
Netherlands	48.8	57.4	+18%
New Zealand	63.4	65.0	+2%
Norway	72.3	71.1	–2%
Portugal	58.2	62.0	+6%
Spain	37.7	44.1	+17%
Sweden	79.4	74.4	–6%
Switzerland	57.3	67.5	+18%
UK	62.4	66.2	+6%
USA	66.2	70.5	+6%

TABLE 5.2: FEMALE EMPLOYMENT RATE BY MALE EARNINGS
DECILE GROUPS

Husband's Position in the Earnings Distribution	Employment Rate of Wives 1987 (%)	Employment Rate of Wives 1994 (%)	Proportional Change in Employment Rate of Wives 1987–1994
First Decile	24.6	30.8	+25%
Second Decile	16.6	45.7	+175%
Third Decile	18.6	45.0	+141%
Fourth Decile	20.8	43.7	+110%
Fifth Decile	17.8	43.2	+143%
Sixth Decile	26.7	47.5	+78%
Seventh Decile	19.0	42.0	+121%
Eighth Decile	28.3	42.9	+52%
Ninth Decile	31.7	38.1	+20%
Tenth Decile	23.4	28.5	+22%
Husband unemployed	20.1	16.7	–17%

Source: Callan, Nolan, O'Neill and Sweetman (1999, forthcoming).

We see that in 1987 employment rates were higher for women married to husbands with above average earnings. In 1987 about 19 per cent of women married to men with below average income were employees, compared with 25 per cent for women married to men with above average earnings. While female employment rates increased between 1987 and 1994 throughout the male earnings distribution, the bulk of the change in employment rates was concentrated among women married to men with below average earnings. By 1994, the relative female employment rates by husbands earnings had reversed: the employment rates were now 42 per cent where the husband had below average earnings and 40 per cent where he had above average earnings. The only group not to experience an increase in employment rates were women married to unemployed men, for whom the employment rate fell from 20 per cent to 17 per cent.

Women and Low Pay

A variety of approaches can be used to define and measure low pay (for example, CERC, 1991, OECD, 1996; Nolan, 1993 discusses approaches previously applied to Irish data). The method which is most widely used, and which we follow, is to derive the low pay threshold as half or two-thirds of median earnings. It can then make a considerable difference whether one focuses on all workers or on full-time employees only, and on hourly or weekly earnings. The OECD in its recent study for example defined low-paid workers as full-time workers who earn less than two-thirds of the median weekly earnings for full-time workers. Since our interest is in female employees and a significant proportion of these are part-timers, it is important to include all employees here, and we use as low pay benchmarks both half and two-thirds the median weekly earnings for all employees. The National Minimum Wage Commission in its recent report (1998) recommended a national hourly minimum wage set at two-thirds of the median. We draw in this section on Nolan's report for that Commission, published as Volume 2 of its Report (1998b).

As background, Table 5.3 first shows the composition of all employees in the 1994 ESRI survey by gender and age.

TABLE 5.3: SEX COMPOSITION OF EMPLOYEES BY AGE GROUP, 1994

	Males		**Females**		**All**
	% of All Males	*% of Total Sample*	*% of All Females*	*% of Total Sample*	*% of Total Sample*
Under 18	1.2	0.6	0.2	0.1	0.7
18 under 21	6.0	3.5	5.8	2.4	5.9
21 under 25	11.0	6.5	17.1	7.0	13.5
25 under 35	27.7	16.4	32.2	13.1	29.6
35 under 45	27.1	16.1	22.5	9.2	25.2
45 under 55	19.0	11.3	15.4	6.3	17.5
55 and over	8.0	4.8	6.8	2.8	7.5
All	100.0	59.3	100.0	40.7	100.0

We see that 59 per cent of employees were men and 41 per cent women. Female employees are more heavily concentrated in the younger age groups, with 23 per cent aged under 25 and 55 per cent under 35 compared with 18 per cent and 46 per cent respectively for men.

Table 5.4 now shows the percentage of employees with earnings below the hourly low pay thresholds in 1994 and in 1987. We see first that the percentage of all employees below half the median was virtually unchanged between 1987 and 1994, at 11 per cent, while the percentage below two-thirds of the hourly median rose from 20 per cent to 23 per cent. A comparison with other countries for whom the OECD has produced results, covering full-time employees only, shows that Ireland has one of the highest levels of low pay of any OECD country (see Barrett, Callan and Nolan, 1998).

TABLE 5.4: PERCENTAGE OF EMPLOYEES BELOW LOW PAY THRESHOLDS, 1987 AND 1994

	1987	1994
	% Below Threshold	
50% of median hourly earnings	11.0	11.4
66% of median hourly earnings	19.8	23.0

Against this background, Table 5.5 shows the risk and incidence of low pay by gender in 1994. We see that women face a substantially higher risk of being low paid than men — 30 per cent of women compared with 18 per cent of men are below the higher cut-off. The second half of the table shows that women therefore account for 52–54 per cent of those experiencing low pay, although as we saw earlier only 41 per cent of all employees are women.

TABLE 5.5: LOW PAY BY GENDER, 1994

	Hourly Earnings Cut-off	
	Half median	*Two-thirds median*
	% Below Cut-off	
Male	9.2	17.8
Female	14.6	30.5
All	11.4	23.0
	% of All Those Below Cut-off	
Male	47.9	45.9
Female	52.1	54.1
All	100.0	100.0

Table 5.6 looks at the risk of low pay by age and sex together. This shows that under the age of 25, there is little or no difference between men and women in the probability of being low paid. It is women aged 25 or over, and particularly those aged 35 or over, who face a much higher risk of being in low pay than men of the same age. For example, 25 per cent of women employees aged between 35 and 44 compared with only seven per cent of men are below two-thirds of the median. For both men and women, the risk of being low paid is highest for the younger age groups, but the gap between young workers and the rest is much smaller for women than men. As a result, women aged 25 or over account for about one-third of all employees, and about the same proportion of the low paid. Men aged 25 or over, by contrast, account for only 15–20 per cent of the low paid, although they constitute almost half of all employees.

Low-paid women are also more likely to be married than low-paid men. With the two-thirds median threshold, for example, 40 per cent of low-paid women compared with 24 per cent of low-paid men are married. This comes about primarily because more low-paid women are in the older age groups, although even within age groups a slightly higher proportion of low-paid women than men are married.

TABLE 5.6: PERCENTAGE LOW PAID BY GENDER AND AGE

	% Below Hourly Earnings Cut-off	
	Half median	*Two-thirds median*
Under 18		
Men	93.8	100.0
Women	57.4	100.0
18 under 21		
Men	46.2	75.0
Women	53.7	78.0
21 under 25		
Men	22.6	45.7
Women	19.4	46.5
25 under 35		
Men	4.8	12.0
Women	8.2	18.6
35 under 45		
Men	2.7	7.2
Women	11.8	24.8
45 under 55		
Men	2.4	6.3
Women	15.0	29.7
55 and over		
Men	4.5	8.8
Women	6.1	24.8

The part-time/full-time distinction is of major importance in the context of low pay, particularly for women. There are different ways of categorising employees as full-time versus part-time: internationally a cut-off of 30 hours is widely used, while in the Irish context an 18 hour threshold is used for some purposes within the social insurance system. In 1994, seven per cent of employees in the ESRI sample worked fewer than 18 hours per week, and 16 per cent worked fewer than 30 hours. The percentage working part-time is much higher for women than men, with 30 per cent of female employees working fewer than 30 hours compared with six per cent for men. This differential is predominantly in the older age groups, with more than 40 per cent of all female employees aged over 35 working fewer than 30 hours compared with under six per cent of men in that age group.

The risk of being low paid is considerably higher for part-time than full-time employees: 49 per cent of those working under 18 hours, and 36 per cent of those working under 30 hours, are below two-thirds of the median compared with 20 per cent of those working 30 hours or more. The fact that women are much more likely than men to be working part-time thus contributes significantly to their higher overall risk of being low paid.

It is also the case however that both among part-time employees and among full-time employees, women face a higher risk of being low paid in hourly terms than men. Table 5.7 shows, for example, that 38 per cent of women working under 30 hours, compared with 30 per cent of men fall below two-thirds of the median. For those working 30 hours or more the extent of low pay is less but the gap between men and women is as wide, with 27 per cent of women compared with 17 per cent of men falling below that cut-off.

While most low-paid part-time workers are indeed women, part-timers do not dominate among low-paid women. Table 5.7 also shows that women working 30 hours or more account for one-third of all employees below two-thirds of the median, whereas women working fewer than 30 hours account for one-fifth.

TABLE 5.7: LOW PAY FOR FULL-TIME AND PART-TIME WOMEN
VERSUS MEN, 1994

	% Below Hourly Earnings Cut-off			
	Half median		*Two-thirds median*	
	Male	*Female*	*Male*	*Female*
Under 18 hours	19.0	24.4	39.2	51.3
Under 30 hours	16.5	18.3	30.0	38.3
30 or more hours	8.7	13.0	17.0	27.2
	% of All Below Cut-off			
	Male	*Female*	*Male*	*Female*
Under 18 hours	2.1	12.2	2.2	12.7
Under 30 hours	5.1	19.6	4.5	20.3
30 or more hours	42.8	32.6	41.3	33.8

Low Pay among Women and Household Poverty

Low pay affects individual earners and is of concern in itself from
that perspective. It may or may not produce poverty for families or
households depending on the nature of the households in which
the low-paid earners live and the extent to which there are other
sources of income for those households. We now analyse the extent to which low pay among women and household poverty overlap: the extent to which low-paid women are in poor households.
Resources may not actually be shared within the household/family
so as to equalise living standards, and low pay may affect the living
standards of the individual earner, irrespective of the situation of
the household in which he or she lives. The intra-household distribution of resources and living standards is explored in the next
chapter, but here our interest is in the overall situation of the
households in which low-paid women live.

For this purpose, as in previous work we measure household
poverty by first comparing total disposable household income with
relative income poverty lines constructed as 50 per cent and 60
per cent of average household income in the sample. Current income alone may not however accurately reflect a household's living standards, which will be influenced by resources over a much
longer period. Measures combining information on income and

indicators of deprivation have therefore been developed from the 1987 and 1994 surveys. A set of eight items or activities was identified from a more extensive list as representing basic deprivation and suitable to serve as an indicator of underlying generalised deprivation. (For example, being able to afford new rather than second-hand clothes or a warm overcoat.) In measuring poverty we thus also look at households below the 60 per cent relative income lines and experiencing such basic forms of deprivation (see Callan *et al*, 1996; Nolan and Whelan, 1996; the full range of deprivation indicators in the surveys is discussed in more detail in Chapter 6).

Since a given income will provide a different living standard to the individuals in a large versus a small household, equivalence scales are widely used to adjust for differences in household size and composition, with actual household income being divided by the number of equivalent adults in the household. There is no consensus as to which method for estimating these scales is most satisfactory, and a variety of equivalence scales has been used in research on Ireland and in cross-country studies. Here we again employ an equivalence scale which attributes a value of 1 to the first adult, 0.66 to each additional adult, and 0.33 to each child (aged under 14); using alternatives scales widely employed in international comparisons such as 1/0.7/0.5 or 1/0.5/0.3 does not affect the results we present.

As background to the relationship between low pay for women and household poverty, it is important to note that in 1994, only about 12–15 per cent of poor households contained an employee — whether male or female, low paid or not. The low income population in Ireland is currently dominated by households relying primarily on social security transfers, and to a much more limited extent income from self-employment (including farming) or occupational pensions, rather than employee earnings. The same is true of households on low income and experiencing basic deprivation.

Table 5.8 now shows the percentage of low-paid women and low-paid men who are in poor households, with the latter identified using relative income poverty lines or a combination of income and deprivation criteria. (Drawing on previous work, the latter could be in terms of the numbers below either the 50 per cent or 60 per cent income line and experiencing what we have termed "basic deprivation"; we concentrate here for convenience

on the higher income cut-off.) We see first that the overall degree
of overlap between low pay and household poverty is quite limited.
Using the "half median" low pay threshold, 11 per cent of the low
paid are in households below half average income, 23 per cent are
in households below the 60 per cent line, and 10 per cent are in
households below that line and experiencing basic deprivation.
Using the higher two-thirds median earnings threshold, a smaller
proportion of the low paid are in poor households.

TABLE 5.8: PERCENTAGE OF LOW-PAID INDIVIDUALS IN POOR
HOUSEHOLDS BY GENDER, 1994

Household Poverty Measure	% of Low-Paid Individuals in Poor Households					
	Below half median			*Below two-thirds median*		
	Men	*Women*	*All*	*Men*	*Women*	*All*
Below 50% line	11.4	10.6	11.0	7.5	6.0	6.7
Below 60% line	26.4	20.1	23.1	19.4	13.6	16.2
Below 60% line + experiencing basic deprivation	11.9	9.2	10.5	9.9	5.7	7.6

Focusing on gender, we then see that a smaller proportion of low-
paid women than low-paid men are in poor households; the gap is
marginal for some of the low pay/poverty measure combinations,
but more pronounced for others. The overlap between low pay and
household poverty is itself highest with the 60 per cent income
line and the half median low pay threshold. This combination of
measures shows one in five low-paid women in a poor household,
and one in four low-paid men.

Looking at the overlap from a household perspective, at most
about 10 per cent of poor households contain a low-paid employee,
and about half that number contain a low-paid woman. This is
primarily because, as we have seen, most poor households do not

contain an employee, whether low-paid or otherwise.[1] This reflects first the fact that the low pay thresholds are substantially higher than the relative poverty lines for a single adult or a couple, so a household might not be below the lines even if relying entirely on such earnings.[2] Secondly, many households containing a low-paid individual are not depending entirely or even primarily on his/her earnings, they have other earners or recipients of social welfare transfers. This is particularly likely to be the case where the low-paid individual is a young adult living in the parental home or a married woman. A limited overlap between low pay and poverty is thus a common finding in UK and US studies such as Layard, Piachaud and Stewart (1978), Bazen (1988), Burkhauser and Finnegan (1989), Sutherland (1995). The precise extent of the overlap depends on the way in which low pay and poverty are measured, but the broad message is similar.

However, low pay in general and low pay for women in particular still affects a substantial proportion of that minority of poor households which do contain an employee, and is therefore highly relevant to the position of the "working poor". Table 5.9 shows that about 55 per cent of the employees who are in poor households have earnings below the two-thirds median threshold. Female employees living in poor households are generally even more likely to be low paid: two-thirds of the female employees in households below the 60 per cent relative income line are themselves earning less than two-thirds of the median.

---

[1] This pattern is not altered by using the narrower family/tax unit of single adult or couple with dependent children rather than the household as recipient unit in measuring poverty.

[2] In 1994, for example, the two-thirds of median hourly earnings threshold corresponded to about £160 per week gross, which for a single person would be about £124 net, whereas even the 60 per cent relative income line was only about £80 for a single person.

TABLE 5.9: PERCENTAGE OF EMPLOYEES IN POOR HOUSEHOLDS
WHO ARE LOW PAID BY GENDER, 1994

Household Poverty Measure	% of the Employees in Poor Households Who are Low Paid					
	Below half median			*Below two-thirds median*		
	Men	*Women*	*All*	*Men*	*Women*	*All*
Below 50% line	40.9	53.1	46.2	51.6	63.1	56.7
Below 60% line	31.9	47.3	37.4	45.3	66.9	53.1
Below 60% line + experiencing basic deprivation	36.0	44.5	39.5	58.7	57.5	58.2

Focusing on the low-paid women who are in poor households, Table 5.10 shows that (based on two-thirds of the median) 55-60 per cent are married, and 30–40 per cent are aged under 25. Compared with all low-paid women, this means a relatively high proportion of the low-paid women in poor households are married (or cohabiting), and if anything a relatively low proportion are in the younger age groups. The most striking characteristic of low-paid women who are in poor households is however the very high proportion — up to three-quarters compared with 38 per cent of all low-paid women — working under 30 hours a week.

It is also worth emphasising that even if many low-paid individuals are not in households below the poverty lines, their incomes may be playing a crucial role in keeping the household out of poverty. We have already seen in earlier chapters that the poverty risk for different types of households is significantly influenced by the number of members in paid employment. We can also illustrate here the impact of the earnings of low-paid workers on the position of their households vis-à-vis the income poverty lines by a crude but revealing exercise. This involves simply deducting the net pay of the low-paid individual from the disposable income of the household

TABLE 5.10: CHARACTERISTICS OF LOW-PAID WOMEN EMPLOYEES IN POOR HOUSEHOLDS

	Women Employees Below Two-thirds Median		
	% part-time (under 30 hours)	*% married / cohabiting*	*% under 25*
In household below 50% line	74.7	59.0	29.5
In household below 60% line	58.5	54.2	34.3
In household below 60% line + experiencing basic deprivation	60.7	54.6	41.5
All women below two-thirds median	37.5	40.5	41.6

and then comparing that reduced income with the relative poverty lines. Table 5.11 shows how often this would bring the households containing low-paid individuals (below two-thirds of the median) below the 50 per cent or 60 per cent poverty lines.[3]

TABLE 5.11: POVERTY RATES FOR HOUSEHOLDS OF LOW-PAID EMPLOYEES IN THE ABSENCE OF THEIR EARNINGS

Household Poverty Measure	% of Low-paid Individuals in Households Above Poverty Line Which Would Be Below it Without Earnings from Low-paid Employment			
	Men	*Women*		
		All	*Married / Cohabiting*	*Widowed, Separated, Divorced*	*Single*
Below 50% line	37.8	22.2	13.6	50.5	24.3
Below 60% line	36.0	24.3	11.9	44.7	31.4

[3] Such an exercise for the combined income plus deprivation criteria would be much more complex, since it would involve predicting the deprivation scores of households with reduced income.

We see that for both low-paid men and women, a substantial proportion are in households above the poverty lines but which would be below those lines if the "low pay" was not coming into the household. This is the case for over one-third of all low-paid men, and 22–24 per cent of all low-paid women, whether the 50 per cent or 60 per cent poverty line is used. Analysing low-paid women by marital status, the table also shows that about half the low-paid women who are widowed, separated or divorced are in households which would fall below the income lines without their earnings. The corresponding figure for single women is 24–31 per cent, while for married or cohabiting women it is about 13 per cent.

Women's Employment and Psychological Distress

Seeking to participate in the paid labour force may have implications not just for the income of women and their households, it can also have a whole range of effects on individual and familial well-being. As a contribution towards opening up this enormously complex area, we look here at a measure of psychological distress, and how it differs between male and female employees and unemployed. This is a topic already addressed using data from the 1987 ESRI survey in Whelan, Hannan and Creighton (1991); here we present some new results from the 1994 Living in Ireland Survey, drawing on the more extensive analysis in Whelan, Gallie, and McGinnity (1998).

The measure of psychological distress used is the 12-item version of Goldberg's General Health Questionnaire (GHQ). The items are designed to give information about the respondent's current mental state, and have been carefully chosen to discriminate between respondent's likelihood of being assessed as a non-psychotic psychiatric case. The items are:

A. Been able to concentrate on whatever you are doing.

B. Lost much sleep over worry.

C. Felt that you are playing a useful part in things.

D. Felt constantly under strain.

E. Felt capable of making decisions.

F. Felt you couldn't overcome your difficulties.

G. Been able to enjoy your normal day-to-day activities.

H. Been feeling unhappy and distressed.

I. Been able to face up to your problems.

J. Been losing confidence in yourself.

K. Been feeling reasonably happy all things considered.

L. Been thinking of yourself as a worthless person.

Generally, items involving positive feelings (e.g. A, C, E etc.) have the response set: "more than usual", "same as usual", "less than usual", "much less than usual", and those replying less or much less than usual are scored as experiencing some degree of distress. Items expressing negative feelings (e.g. B, D, F) have the response set: "not at all", "no more than usual", "rather more than usual", "much more than usual", and responses of rather or much more than usual are taken as indicating distress.

Table 5.12 shows mean GHQ scores for male and female employees and unemployed in the 1994 ESRI survey. As in 1987, we see that, among employees, women have higher GHQ scores than men, whereas among the unemployed the opposite is true.

TABLE 5.12: MEAN GHQ SCORE BY GENDER AND EMPLOYMENT STATUS, 1994

	Women	Men	Total
Employees	1.40	1.08	1.20
Unemployed	2.12	3.15	2.90

Table 5.13 then takes marital status into account. This reveals that among employees, women have higher mean GHQ scores than men whether single or married, and among the unemployed women have lower GHQ scores than men whether single or married. Among employees, married people have lower GHQ scores. For the unemployed, on the other hand, marriage is associated with higher levels of distress for men, but lower levels for women.

TABLE 5.13: GHQ SCORE BY GENDER, EMPLOYMENT STATUS AND MARITAL STATUS, 1994

	Employees		Unemployed	
	Men	*Women*	*Men*	*Women*
Married	0.88	1.19	3.38	1.89
Single	1.40	1.60	2.90	2.17

Focusing on those who are married only, Table 5.14 now compares GHQ scores for male and female employees and unemployed cross-tabulated by whether their spouse is at work or unemployed. We see that for men, GHQ scores are lower when the wife is at work than when she is unemployed. This is also the case for women employees, in fact the effect is more pronounced. However, for unemployed women GHQ scores are actually lower when their husband is unemployed than when he is at work.

TABLE 5.14: MEAN GHQ SCORE BY GENDER AND EMPLOYMENT STATUS AND WHETHER PARTNER IS AT WORK

	Partner at Work		Partner Not at Work	
	Men	*Women*	*Men*	*Women*
Employees	0.82	1.17	1.04	1.59
Unemployed	2.59	2.73	2.89	1.55

Another factor one might expect to influence GHQ scores is the presence or absence of children. Table 5.15 shows that presence of children is associated with increased GHQ scores for men. In particular, unemployed men with children have significantly higher GHQ scores than those without children. For women, on the other hand, it is those without children who have the higher GHQ scores though the difference is much less pronounced than for men, and for women employees is marginal.

TABLE 5.15: MEAN GHQ SCORE BY GENDER, UNEMPLOYMENT
STATUS, AND HAVING CHILDREN (MARRIED RESPONDENTS ONLY)

	Men		**Women**	
	Employee	*Unemployed*	*Employee*	*Unemployed*
No Children	0.73	2.50	1.22	2.06
Children	0.91	3.45	1.18	1.84

Barriers to Women's Employment

Given the importance of women's earnings in lifting or keeping
households out of poverty, it is necessary to also consider briefly the
range of barriers facing women seeking to take up paid employment. Key obstacles are in the area of wage levels, childcare,
training and education and the tax and social welfare system.

The most obvious barrier to taking up employment may simply
be the unavailability of jobs at a wage level that would be attractive, given the tax and welfare system and the individual's circumstances. The introduction of a national hourly minimum wage
along the lines recommended by the Minimum Wage Commission
would clearly be a radical change in the policy environment in this
respect, and it is worth considering its likely impact on women.
Because women, as we have seen, constitute a majority of all low-
paid employees, they would also be affected disproportionately by
a minimum wage. This would be true of any negative impact on
employment prospects, but also of any gains from increased
earnings level.

A minimum wage set at two-thirds of median hourly earnings
(with lower rates for those aged under 18), along the lines recommended by the National Minimum Wage Commission in its recent
report (1998), would affect about 22 per cent of all employees (see
National Minimum Wage Commission Report, Volume 2, by B.
Nolan 1998). Over half — 55 per cent — of these employees would
be women. The first-round effects, before any behavioural responses by employers or employees (actual or potential), would be
to increase the gross (hourly or weekly) earnings of the low-paid
by an average of 39 per cent: this average increase would be very
much the same for men and women. While most of those affected
are not in poor households, some of the minority who are could see

their households lifted out of poverty by the minimum wage. The increase in gross earnings it would produce, if that were not taxed and other income of the household was unaffected, would be sufficient to cut the numbers of low paid in households below the 60 per cent poverty line by half.

In practice, of course, some of that increase in gross income could be taxed away, while social welfare transfers would also fall in some instances (notably where Family Income Supplement is being received). A comprehensive simulation of the first-round effects of a minimum wage taking these tax and benefit effects into account would have to be carried out using a tax/benefit simulation model such as the SWITCH model developed at the ESRI. Further, the crucial issue of the likely effects of a minimum wage at the recommended level on employment needs to be carefully assessed. Women make up the majority of the potential beneficiaries from the minimum wage, but it is also their jobs that would be most at risk from a minimum wage set at too high a level.

The availability and cost of childcare currently act as a major barrier to participation by women in the paid labour force. This has been repeatedly recognised, most recently by the Second Commission on the Status of Women (1993) and the Commission on the Family (1998). It is instructive to note, however, the absence of consensus on how best to tackle the problem. The Commission on the Family thus discussed several alternative policy options, while emphasizing the role of the state in providing financial support for childcare in or outside the home in the early years. The fact that a range of objectives underlie child income support policy is fundamental: the aim is not simply or solely to faciltate employment outside the home or financial independence of women, however important that might be. The alleviation of poverty among children is also a central concern, as is the sharing across the community of some of the costs of raising children, and the position of women in the home must also be taken into account.

The discussion of alternative policy options in, for example, Nolan (1993) and Fahey (1998) brings out the fact that either child tax allowances in the income tax system or tax allowances for paid childcare, although superficially attractive, would be regressive and have little impact on poor families. Alternative strategies, including direct provision of quality childcare (with priority given to disadvantaged communities) and universal support for children through child benefit, are preferable from an anti-poverty perspective.

Linked to childcare responsibilities, women seeking to re-enter the labour force after a period working full-time in the home also face a number of barriers, particularly with respect to training. Married women and lone parents have been more successful in obtaining access to active labour market programmes in recent years than heretofore, but not for the most part those more closely linked to the labour market. Research has shown that it is programmes of this sort — that is, training in specific employable skills and temporary employment subsidies for "real jobs" — which are most effective in promoting participants' job prospects (O'Connell and McGinnity, 1997). General training or direct employment schemes are of themselves unlikely to significantly improve the job prospects of participants. They must be followed by progression to more advanced schemes with better linkages with the open labour market (O'Connell, 1998). A recent report on the impact of Community Employment (Murphy, Deloitte and Touche, 1998) does suggest that job placement rates of participants have improved in recent years, but also that market oriented training programmes such as Specific Skills and Job Training are a great deal more effective in those terms.

Aspects of both the tax and social welfare systems may also act as barriers to women taking up paid employment. As far as the tax system is concerned, the income tax treatment of couples is particularly problematic. Because both personal allowances and tax bands are transferable from a non-working to a working spouse, a non-working spouse in that situation is likely to effectively face the top tax rate on prospective earnings. That top tax rate is currently 46 per cent, and employee social insurance contributions bring the effective marginal tax rate facing non-working spouses of those in employment above 50 per cent. Structural reform of the income tax system in this respect, to restrict the transferability of bands and/or allowances, would have a positive impact on incentives facing a non-working spouse while also potentially freeing up resources which could be directed more effectively towards families with children.

As far as the social welfare system is concerned, a variety of disincentives to taking up paid employment can face married women or lone parents. These are most pronounced for those in receipt of means-tested social assistance payments. It is important to note that there have been some significant improvements in this respect in recent years. The 1997 Budget saw the introduction of tapered withdrawal of the additional payments for "adult dependants" as the earnings of the dependent spouse increase.[4] The recent move to assessing Family Income Supplement on a net basis should also help to limit the impact of withdrawal of benefits as the earnings of either spouse increase. In addition, the means test for lone parents was restructured with integration of Lone Parent Allowance, Widower's Pension, Deserted Wife's Benefit, etc. into one payment, the One Parent Family Payment, from January 1998. The new means test is structured with the explicit objective of providing incentives to lone parents to seek employment. Key elements are that all gross earnings up to a ceiling (currently £6,000 per annum) are disregarded, and half the earnings in excess of that figure are also disregarded.

However, in the case of lone parents two important issues still arise with respect to this new structure. The first is that no account is taken of childcare costs in assessing means. The second is that the Supplementary Welfare Allowance Rent Allowance for those in private rented accommodation is withdrawn pound for pound as earnings rise. McCashin (1997) states that this "may be critical from a labour market perspective, as it impinges on large numbers of lone parent families" (p. 51). Both issues impinge more generally on women in families depending on social welfare, as do the broader disincentive problems created by the tax and social welfare system in combination, examined in great detail in for example the Report of the Expert Group on Integrating Tax and Social Welfare (1996). The broad reform strategy required to promote disincentives includes targeted tax

---

[4] Up to that point, no additional payment was payable if spouse earned more than £60; now, some payment retained as earnings go from £60 to £90.

reductions for those on low pay, seeking to reduce rather than increase the role of means testing in the social welfare system, and providing more of the state's support for children through universal Child Benefit. Such a strategy could substantially ease the barriers to participation in the paid labour force currently facing women.

Conclusions

The extent and nature of women's participation in the paid labour force is of crucial importance for women and poverty. This chapter began by documenting recent trends in women's participation in the paid labour force. Since the mid-1980s, the increase in the overall participation rate for Irish women has outstripped that in most OECD countries, though from a low base. The increase in the numbers of Irish women at work outside the home in the 1990s exceeded that in the previous 20 years. Analysis of the ESRI samples for 1987 and 1994 showed that the percentage of married women working as employees rose from 22 per cent to 34 per cent over that period. This increase was particularly pronounced for women married to men on below-average earnings, but for women married to unemployed men the percentage in employment actually fell.

As in most other industrialised countries, women are much more likely than men to be working for low levels of pay. (The differentials between male and female earnings throughout the distribution are being examined in a separate study using the same data base.) We then looked in some detail at the position of women in the 1994 ESRI survey working as employees, analysing the extent to which their earnings fall below commonly-used low pay benchmarks. This showed that women comprised 41 per cent of all employees but 54 per cent of those earning below two-thirds of median hourly earnings. For those aged under 25, there was little difference between men and women in the proportion of low paid. Women aged 25 or over, and particularly those aged 35 or over, face a much higher risk of being in low pay than men of the same age. For example, 25 per cent of women employees between the ages of 35 and 44 earned less than two-thirds of the median, compared with only seven per cent of men in that age range.

Women working part-time are also particularly likely to be low paid.

We then looked at how many of the women who are low paid also live in poor households, and the contribution which low paid women's earnings make to keeping households out of poverty. The results showed first that the overall degree of overlap between low pay and poverty, for men or women, was quite limited. At most only about 16 per cent of low-paid individuals were members of households below the highest, 60 per cent relative income poverty line. Focusing on this minority of the low paid, a higher proportion of low-paid men than women were seen to be in poor households.

However, low pay in general and low pay for women in particular still affects a substantial proportion of that minority of poor households which do contain an employee, and is therefore highly relevant to the position of the "working poor". About 55 per cent of the employees who are in poor households have earnings below two-thirds of the median. Female employees living in poor households are generally even more likely to be low paid: two-thirds of the female employees in households below the 60 per cent relative income line are themselves earning less than two-thirds of the median. The low-paid women who are living in poor households are particularly likely to be working part-time. Again for both low-paid men and women, we also saw that a substantial proportion are in non-poor households which would be below the poverty lines if those low earnings were not coming into the household.

Women's participation in the employed labour force has widespread effects on themselves and their families beyond the income earned. One aspect of this broader context that we were able to examine here was the impact of unemployment versus employment on psychological distress levels for men versus women. The measure of psychological distress used was the General Health Questionnaire or GHQ, which was included in the 1987 and 1994 ESRI surveys. The results presented here for 1994, like Whelan, Hannan and Creighton (1991) findings for 1987, showed that among employees women had higher GHQ scores — and thus higher levels of "stress" — than men. Among the unemployed, on the other hand, the opposite was true: women had lower stress levels on average than men. Among employees, both married men and married women had lower GHQ scores than their unmarried counterparts. For the unemployed, on the other hand, marriage is associated with higher levels of distress for men but with lower levels for women. Further, GHQ scores for married persons are in general lower when their partner is at work rather than unemployed, but for unemployed women stress levels are actually lower when their husband is unemployed than when he is at work.

Finally, the chapter looked at some of the obstacles facing women who want to take up paid employment. These relate particularly to the wages paid by the jobs on offer, childcare, training and education and disincentives built into the tax and social welfare systems. The introduction of a national hourly minimum wage along the lines recommended by the National Minimum Wage Commission would clearly be a radical change in the labour market in this respect. Women make up the majority of the potential beneficiaries from a minimum wage along the lines recommended by the National Minimum Wage Commission, but it is also their jobs that would be most at risk from a minimum wage set at too high a level.

The availability and cost of childcare currently act as a major barrier to participation by women in the paid labour force. However, in addition to facilitating employment outside the home and the financial independence of women, policy in this complex area must also focus on the alleviation of poverty among children, sharing across the community of some of the costs of raising children, and the position of women in the home. Among the range of alternative policy options, child tax allowances in the income tax system or tax allowances for paid childcare would be regressive and have little impact on poor families. Alternative strategies, including direct provision of quality childcare (with priority given to disadvantaged communities) and universal support for children through child benefit, are preferable from an anti-poverty perspective.

Women seeking to re-enter the labour force after a period working full-time in the home also face barriers with respect to training. Recent research has shown that programmes linked closely to the labour market are the most effective in promoting participants' job prospects: general training or direct employment schemes are of themselves unlikely to do so. The crucial issue for women seeking to re-enter the labour market is thus not simply participation in programmes but progression to more advanced schemes with better linkages with the open labour market (O'Connell, 1998).

Aspects of both the tax and social welfare systems also act as barriers to women taking up paid employment. Full transferability of personal allowances and tax bands from a non-working to a working spouse means that the former faces a high tax rate on prospective earnings. A variety of disincentives to taking up paid employment can face married women or lone parents relying on social welfare transfers, particularly means-tested social assistance payments. There have been some significant improvements in this respect in recent years, notably tapered withdrawal of additional payments for "adult dependants" as the earnings of the dependent spouse increase, the recent move to assessing Family Income Supplement on a net basis, and the restructuring of the means test for lone parents. However, particular problems still arise in terms of the treatment of childcare costs in assessing means, and the pound for pound withdrawal of rent allowance as earnings rise. The broader disincentive problems created by the tax and social welfare system in combination could be tackled by targeting tax reductions on the low paid, reducing the role of means testing in the social welfare system, and providing more of the state's support for children through universal child benefit. Such a strategy could help to substantially ease the barriers to participation in the paid labour force currently facing women.

Chapter 6

INTRA-HOUSEHOLD DISTRIBUTION AND WOMEN'S POVERTY

Introduction

Conventional methods of analysis of poverty and income inequality take the household or the narrower family as the income recipient unit, and assume resources are shared so that each individual in a given household/family has the same standard of living. Assuming equal living standards within the household in measuring poverty means that either all members of a given household will be counted as poor or all will be counted as non-poor, and each member of a poor household will be assessed as equally poor. Critics argue that the result is that women's poverty within households above the poverty line remains hidden, as does the extent to which women within poor households disproportionately suffer the consequences in terms of reduced consumption (Millar and Glendinning, 1987). Ignoring the within-household distribution in this way has also been criticised on the basis that it obscures gender differences in the causes and experience of poverty, but these criticisms have as yet had little impact on mainstream poverty measurement practice (Jenkins, 1991).

Rottman's (1993) study for the Combat Poverty Agency of the way resources are distributed within Irish households sought to open up the household "black box". It focused on household management/allocation systems — for example where one person is responsible for all routine purchases from a "kitty", or where there is shared management or independent management by the two spouses. It also included an exploratory analysis of the consequences that alternative allocation systems had for the standard of living enjoyed by different family members, but this was based on the very limited set of "outcome" measures, such as access to personal spending money, which were in the data. Here our aim is to build on this work by employing richer data on non-monetary indicators of deprivation to directly measure deprivation at the level of the individual and explore differences in deprivation between individuals in the same household. (Unfortunately, we do not have the information on household allocation systems which was available to Rottman, and so cannot extend our analysis to the relationships between intra-household inequalities and those systems.)

The items on which we have information were not chosen with intra-household differences in living standards and deprivation as the primary focus, nor was the way the data was collected structured with that issue to the forefront. While the indicators thus have limitations for present purposes, this is itself a necessary first step to building bridges between measurement of deprivation at household and at intra-household levels. Here we first describe the indicators available. We then summarise the findings from Cantillon and Nolan's (1998) comparison of deprivation among wives and their husbands based on these indicators. Finally, we go on to adopt an alternative perspective on the distribution of resources within the household, using the same set of indicators but focusing on the determinants of deprivation at individual level.

The Data

The data employed here are from the 1987 ESRI Survey because this, unlike the 1994 Living in Ireland Survey, sought information on non-monetary indicators of lifestyle and deprivation from each adult in sample households. (The 1994 Survey sought this information only from one adult in each household, whoever was completing the household questionnaire.) While it would be desirable to have more up-to-date information, it does not seem likely that the broad scale of intra-household inequalities or their implications for poverty would have changed radically in the intervening years.

The 1987 survey obtained information on the set of indicators of style of living described and analysed in detail in Callan, Nolan and Whelan (1993) and extended in Nolan and Whelan (1996).

The 20 items or activities to be considered as possible indicators of deprivation are listed in Table 6.1. Some of these items will be common to all members of a family or household — for example a fridge or a bath/shower — but some do clearly relate to the individual, while others are more difficult to categorise as familial versus personal. Respondents were asked which of these items they did not have or could not avail of, and also which ones they would like to have but were doing without because of lack of money.

TABLE 6.1: LIFESTYLE ITEMS/ACTIVITIES MEASURED IN 1987 ESRI SURVEY

Item
Refrigerator
Washing machine
Telephone
Car
Colour television
A week's annual holiday away from home (not staying with relatives)
A dry, damp-free dwelling
Heating for the living rooms when it is cold
Central heating in the house
An indoor toilet in the dwelling (not shared with other households)
Bath or shower (not shared with other households)
A meal with meat, chicken or fish every second day
A warm, waterproof overcoat
Two pairs of strong shoes
To be able to save some of one's income regularly
A daily newspaper
A roast meat joint or its equivalent once a week
A hobby or leisure activity
New, not second-hand, clothes
Presents for friends or family once a year

Comparing Deprivation of Wives and their Husbands

Cantillon and Nolan (1998) present an in-depth comparison of the responses of *spouses* in the 1987 survey to these questions, and concentrate on quantifying and analysing any divergences between them. Here we will simply summarise the main findings of that analysis, before moving on to an alternative approach using the broader set of responses of all adults. Table 6.2 shows for each of the 20 items the percentage of couples where both spouses say they do not have the item, the percentage where both say that they do, and the percentage where the spouses differ in their responses about lack/possession of the item. We see that although spouses in most cases gave the same response, for a substantial proportion of the items this was not the case in five per cent or more of cases. Both these results, and the nature of the items themselves, suggest that the items listed in the bottom half of the table are unlikely to have much potential as indicators of individual rather than familial living standards, but the top half do seem to have some such potential.

Concentrating on the ten items which may be considered as potentially personal, summary deprivation indices can be constructed for each individual, with a score of one being added to the index for each item which he or she lacks. Subtracting the husband's score on the ten-item index from that of his wife gives a measure of the "gap" between them.[1] About 46 per cent of couples were found to have a zero gap — husband and wife had identical scores on their individual indices. About 29 per cent have gaps greater than zero, so the wife has a higher deprivation index score than the husband, and 25 per cent have a negative gap, the husband has a higher index score than the wife. We also looked at the more restricted set of the five items which appear most likely to be strictly personal in nature — an overcoat, two pairs of shoes, a hobby or leisure activity, new clothes, and a holiday — and constructed similar indices. About 58 per cent of couples then showed no gap, 17 per cent had a gap in favour of the wife, and 25 per cent had a gap in favour of the husband.

---

[1] Note that here our analysis relates to married rather than cohabiting couples.

TABLE 6.2: SPOUSES' RESPONSES ON 20 STYLE OF LIVING ITEMS

Item	% Neither Say Lacking	% Both Say Lacking	% Spouses Differ
A week's holiday away from home	27.2	62.2	10.6
A meal with meat, chicken or fish every second day	87.9	7.2	5.0
A warm, waterproof overcoat	82.1	6.8	11.1
Two pairs of strong shoes	77.3	9.5	13.2
To be able to save	34.8	49.6	15.5
A daily newspaper	56.3	37.2	6.5
A roast meat joint or equivalent once a week	80.7	11.5	7.8
A hobby or leisure activity	55.6	21.6	22.8
New, not second-hand, clothes	88.5	4.5	6.9
Presents for friends or family once a year	77.1	11.5	11.5
Refrigerator	97.8	1.9	0.3
Washing machine	89.7	9.2	1.2
Telephone	56.3	42.5	1.2
Car	74.5	23.5	2.1
Colour TV	85.2	13.6	1.2
A dry, damp-free dwelling	90.3	6.8	2.8
Heating for the living rooms	97.1	1.0	1.9
Central heating in the house	62	35	3.0
An indoor toilet	96.4	3.4	0.3
Bath/shower	95.8	3.9	0.2

Some of these differences between spouses could arise due to differences in tastes rather than be enforced by resource constraints, so differences between spouses in whether absence of items was attributed to be due to lack of money were also examined. A ten-item deprivation index was again constructed for each individual, with a score of one now being added for each item that the individual lacks *and* states this is because they cannot afford it. Subtracting the husband's from the wife's score, about 54 per cent of couples now had zero gap, 21 per cent had the husband with a higher index score than the wife, and 26 per cent had wives with higher scores than husbands. Compared with the gap measure for the simple lack indices, this meant slightly fewer spouses with diverging scores but again more wives than husbands relatively disadvantaged. This remained true for the corresponding indices for the five "unambiguously personal" items: in that case the gap was zero for 65 per cent of couples, favoured the wife for 14 per cent, and favoured the husband for 21 per cent.

The way these gaps between the wife's and the husband's score on the various summary deprivation indices varied with a range of individual and family characteristics was also analysed. No systematic relationship with household income, social class or age was found, all being insignificant in regressions with the various gap measures as dependent variable. Income (if any) received directly by the wife was found to be statistically significant, women with such an income having lower predicted gaps, but this explained little of the variance in these gaps.

The Determinants of Deprivation at Individual Level

The set of ten non-monetary indicators described in the previous section as largely personal rather than familial can be used not only to compare the position of spouses in terms of deprivation, but also to look at determinants of deprivation at individual level. This may allow us in particular to infer conclusions about the extent to which resources within the family or the household are equitably distributed. As in the comparison of spouses, we use summary deprivation scores constructed with these ten items for each individual as a measure of individual-level deprivation, but now include all those responding to the questions (rather than only spouses). Using these scores as dependent variables, we then analyse which of the very wide range of individual, family and household characteristics on which we have information are significant determinants of individual deprivation scores. We will be particularly interested in the impact of income, and whether it is the income accruing to the individual, the total accruing to his or her family, or the total accruing to the wider household that plays the more important role in influencing the individual's living standards. (The household, as we saw earlier, is conventionally defined as a single person or group of people regularly living in the same accommodation and sharing catering arrangements; the family is then the narrower unit of single person or couple with dependent children, if any.)

We therefore construct from the 1987 ESRI survey a dataset at the level of the individual adult, which has for each adult the following variables:

1. Deprivation as measured by the individual's own responses on the ten "personal" non-monetary indicators;

2. For the individual him or herself: age, sex, marital status, educational attainment, labour force status, career unemployment experience, social class, whether his or her family had great difficulty making ends meet when he or she was growing up, and his or her own income and level of financial savings;

3. Each of these variables for the head of the family to which the individual belongs, together with the composition of the family in terms of number of children, and the total income accruing to the family and its level of financial savings; and

4. Each of these variables for the head of the household to which the individual belongs, together with the composition of the household in terms of number of children, the total income accruing to the household, household financial savings, the value of the house as an asset and whether it is in an urban or rural location.[2]

---

[2] The financial variables — income, savings and the value of the housing asset — are entered in logarithmic form.

These variables, as measured by the responses of the household head, have been shown in previous work to influence the level of deprivation being experienced at household level (see especially Nolan and Whelan, 1996). Here though we are measuring them at each of the three levels, for the individual, the family and the household, and analysing their impact on deprivation measured at the level of the individual. (In order to be able to carry out this test, for the variables relating to the "head" in couple-headed households and families we take the characteristics of the male.) Starting with the encompassing set of all these variables, regression analysis has been used to explore which have a significant impact on individual deprivation scores on the ten-item indices already described. Deleting insignificant variables step by step, the variables that appear significant in explaining individual deprivation scores in the results to date are in Table 6.3.

We see that almost all the variables that are significant in explaining the deprivation scores of individuals are the ones measured at the level of the household. The individual's deprivation score is predicted to be higher where the head is unemployed, away from work due to illness, or in home duties, where he/she has no educational qualification beyond primary level, is chronically ill, has substantial career unemployment experience, and experienced financial difficulty growing up. The individual's deprivation score is predicted to be lower where the head is in the professional/managerial social classes, where the household is in an urban rather than rural area, and the higher the level of household financial savings and the value of the house. The income of the individual does appear as significant and with the expected negative sign, but it has much less impact than the total income of the household, which has a coefficient ten times as great.

This is highly relevant to on-going debates about the most satisfactory income recipient unit to use in measuring poverty and income inequality. In the UK, the nearest thing to regular official poverty statistics for many years were those on "Low Income Families", using the tax/benefit unit and showing the numbers at or below the level of social security safety-net support. In the late

TABLE 6.3: FACTORS INFLUENCING INDIVIDUAL SCORES ON 10-ITEM DEPRIVATION INDEX

Independent Variable	Coefficient (t-value in parentheses)
Individual's own disposable income	−0.04 (2.87)
Household equivalised disposable income	−0.42 (8.57)
Household head's age	−0.006 (2.69)
Household head unemployed	0.66 (6.34)
Household head away from work due to illness	0.48 (4.14)
Spouse of head is at work	−0.10 (1.48)
Household head in home duties	0.37 (3.24)
Household head chronically ill or disabled	0.14 (2.05)
Household head separated or divorced	0.92 (4.90)
Household head career unemployment	1.62 (5.46)
Household head in higher professional/managerial class	−0.46 (5.41)
Household head in lower professional/managerial class	−0.35 (4.49)
Household head has no educational qualifications beyond primary	0.49 (7.88)
Household head's family had financial difficulty when he/she was growing up	0.46 (7.82)
Level of household financial savings	-0.11 (14.71)
Value of house net of outstanding mortgage	−0.06 (8.38)
Urban location	−0.18 (3.20)
Number of children under 18 in household	0.15 (8.55)

1980s these were replaced by the "Households below Average Income Series", which involved *inter alia* a switch to the household as the income recipient unit. This in itself reduced the numbers being counted as on low income, and as a consequence was the subject of considerable debate (see Nolan, 1989; Johnson and Webb, 1989). Our analysis tends to support the argument made by the official UK statisticians at the time (and supported by Nolan, 1989) that, given the choice between the family and the household, using the latter as income recipient unit is likely to more accurately reflect the living standards of household members. Family income does not appear as a significant influence on individual deprivation scores in our results, whereas household income appears as an important influence. As in our previous analyses at household level, however (notably Nolan and Whelan, 1996), current household income is only one of a wide range of variables which affect deprivation, with long-term factors reflecting the accumulation or erosion of resources clearly playing an important part. The fact that individual income has been found here to affect individual deprivation scores, albeit in a rather marginal way, will be the subject of further investigation.

Conclusions

Conventional methods of analysis of poverty and income inequality take the household or the narrower family as the income recipient unit, and assume resources are shared so that each individual in a given household/family has the same standard of living. The concern addressed in this chapter is women's poverty within households above the poverty line that could remain hidden, as could the extent to which women within poor households disproportionately suffer the consequences in terms of reduced consumption. We have sought to investigate the extent of differences within the household by using data on non-monetary indicators of deprivation, from the 1987 ESRI survey, to directly measure deprivation at the level of the individual.

Some of the non-monetary indicators on which we have information refer to items which will be common to all members of a family or household — for example a fridge or a bath/shower. However some do clearly relate to the individual — such as a warm overcoat or a second pair of shoes — while others are more difficult to categorise as familial versus personal. We focused on a set of ten items which to a greater or lesser extent appear to relate to the circumstances of the individual.

Our interest was first in whether wives experience greater deprivation than their husbands, as small-scale studies have suggested they might, because of an unequal distribution of resources within the family where the husband is the sole or main income earner. For a sample of 1,763 couples, differences between spouses in responses on individual items were examined, and divergences in their scores on summary deprivation indices constructed using these items were analysed (drawing on the more detailed presentation in Cantillon and Nolan. 1998).

The results showed that husband and wife gave different answers on whether they had a specific item in between five per cent and 15 per cent of couples. In about 55 per cent of the cases where differences did occur, the wife lacked the item and the husband possessed it. Constructing summary indices of deprivation using these ten items, a divergence in scores between husband and wife was seen in about half the sample couples: in about 56 per cent of these the wife had the higher deprivation score, while in 44 per cent the husband had the higher score. This general pattern was also found using indices constructed with a more restricted set of five items that were more unambiguously personal. The same was true when subjective assessments of respondents as to whether they were doing without items because they could not afford them were used, and when only enforced lack of an item possessed by one's spouse was counted as deprivation. No systematic relationship was found between the difference in the wife's and the husband's score on these summary deprivation indices and either household income, social class, or age. Where the wife had an income of her own the predicted gap was slightly lower, but this explained little of the actual variation we found across couples.

We then used the same set of non-monetary indicators for all individuals in the sample (not just spouses) to analyse the determinants of deprivation at individual level. In particular, we were interested to see whether it was the income accruing to the individual, the total accruing to his or her nuclear family, or the total accruing to the wider household that plays the more important role in influencing the individual's living standards. The results tend to support the argument that, given the choice between the family and the household, using the latter as income recipient unit is likely to more accurately reflect the living standards of household members. Family income does not appear as a significant influence on individual deprivation scores, whereas household income appears as a very important influence. As in previous analyses at household level, however (notably Nolan and Whelan,

1996), current household income is seen to be only one of a wide range of variables which affect deprivation, with long-term factors reflecting the accumulation or erosion of resources clearly also playing an important part.

The deprivation indicators we had available were ones employed in previous poverty studies based on large-scale survey data, designed primarily to reflect the situation of the household. The quite limited imbalance in favour of husbands we found using these indicators does not suggest that conventional poverty measurement practice "misses" substantial numbers of poor women in non-poor households. This suggests in turn that policies directing resources towards poor households are not failing to assist substantial numbers of women outside those households but experiencing a similar level of deprivation.

However, it is important to also bring out the limitations of the measures of deprivation available to us for the analysis of intrahousehold differences, reflecting the fact that this was not the objective for which they were designed. The next stage in exploring these issues will have to be the development of more sensitive indicators of deprivation designed to measure individual living standards and poverty status, which can fit within the framework of traditional poverty research using large samples. This is something that has so far received little attention in the research literature, though insights derived from small-scale qualitative studies would be a valuable input. Availability of information for a large sample on individual incomes and in-depth non-monetary "outcomes" measures, together with the way the household allocates resources (as studied by Rottman, 1993), would be particularly valuable.

It is also important in conclusion to stress that a situation where women do not experience much greater deprivation than men would still be entirely consistent with pervasive sex inequalities and with the concentration among husbands of the power to make major financial decisions. Such a concentration, with consequences for power relationships within the family, can of course be of concern in its own right — apart altogether from its implications for poverty — in a framework which focuses on equity between men and women in the division of roles, responsibilities and power.

Chapter 7

CONCLUSIONS

The Aim of the Study

This study has been concerned with women and poverty in Ireland. The importance of this topic is reflected by the fact that one of the National Anti-Poverty Strategy's guiding principles is "the reduction of inequalities and in particular addressing the gender dimension of poverty" (p. 7). Since a single study cannot hope to deal satisfactorily with all the issues relevant to women and poverty, much less the broader gender inequalities within which they must be seen, we have concentrated on three core issues. These are:

- How and why the risk of poverty for households headed by women versus those headed by couples or men, and the risk of poverty for women versus men, have been changing;

- The extent and nature of low pay for women in employment and how it relates to household poverty; and,

- What non-monetary indicators of deprivation can tell us about the distribution of resources and the extent of "hidden poverty" among women within the household.

All three aspects have featured extensively in both national and international debates and discussions on the causes and implications of poverty for women. The aim of the study has been to enhance understanding on these issues, building on the foundations of previous research, and in doing so to contribute both to current policy formulation and to further development of a gender-focused poverty research agenda for the future.

The Research Background

The feminisation of poverty is a term emanating originally from the USA, used to describe an increase in the proportion of poor households there that are headed by women. The term has also been used more broadly to refer to an increasing proportion of poor adults who are female, also a feature of US experience. Research there has concentrated on factors leading to the rise in the proportion of "female-headed" households (particularly marital breakdown, non-marital births and widowhood), and on the changing composition of those households (in terms of race, marital status and age of the head). While the theme of feminisation of poverty has served as a very useful spur to research, the notion that in households containing a couple the man is taken as head — so "female-headed households" are those where the "head" is a single, divorced, or widowed woman — has been criticised.

As far as the corresponding trends in Ireland are concerned, results from the 1987 ESRI household survey showed the risk of being below income poverty lines declining sharply for female-headed households between 1973 and 1987. As a result, by 1987 female-headed households faced a below-average risk of falling below half mean income and a marginally above-average risk of falling below 60 per cent of that mean, whereas at the start of the period they had a very much higher risk than other households at both these lines. This reflected in particular the substantial improvement over the period in the relative position of the elderly. By contrast, results from the 1994 Living in Ireland Survey showed that between 1987 and 1994 there was a substantial increase in the risk of income poverty facing households headed by a woman, whereas the risk for those headed by a man or a couple was rather stable. Explaining why this occurred has been an important element in the present study.

The gap between male and female wages has been a focus of research internationally and in the Irish case with ESRI survey data. From a poverty perspective, however, it is the concentration of women in low-paid employment rather than the male–female wage gap along the entire spectrum of pay rates that is of primary importance. Nolan (1993) used the 1987 ESRI survey to examine the extent and composition of low pay at that date, bringing out the much higher probability of low pay for women than men employees and the concentration of low-paid women in certain sectors. Nolan's recent study for the National Minimum Wage Commission (1998b) up-dated this picture using the 1994 ESRI survey, and in this study our aim has been to develop this analysis and bring out what it means for poverty among women and the households in which they live.

Most research on poverty relies on income as the measure of living standards or poverty status, and adopts the household as the income sharing unit. This means that either everyone in a given household will be counted as poor, or none of them will be counted as poor. While reliance on the household (and on income) has many advantages, it may mask significant inequalities between household members, and the implications these may have for poverty among women. Rottman's (1993) study for the Combat Poverty Agency looked at the way resources are distributed within households, using results from an ESRI survey carried out in 1989, which contained questions on the way family finances were managed. This allowed households to be classified into different management/allocation systems — for example where one person is responsible for all routine purchases from a "kitty", or there is shared management or independent management by the two spouses. The conclusions reached were that the consequences of how household finances are managed are quite significant for the well-being of individual members, but that — tentatively — the results did not lend credence to the notion that substantial numbers of women and children live in "hidden poverty" in non-poor households. Here we make use of a much broader range of non-monetary indicators of deprivation to explore differences in living standards between individuals within the same household.

The data employed in this study come from two large-scale household surveys carried out by the ESRI: the Survey of Income Distribution, Poverty and Usage of State Services carried out in 1987; and the 1994 Living in Ireland Survey, both described in detail elsewhere.

Increasing Poverty Risk for Female-headed Households

The increasing risk observed between 1987 and 1994 for households headed by a woman rather than a man or couple was our first point of departure. We began by looking at a range of factors that might be expected to influence the risk of poverty for households, and at how the major ones evolved over the period. This showed for example that by 1994, lone mother households contained fewer adults and more children on average than in 1987, and there had been a sizeable drop in the proportion of lone mothers who were widowed rather than never married or divorced/separated. Women living alone were also more likely by 1994 to be single than widowed.

We then drew on these results to inform a more formal regression analysis, aimed at identifying with greater precision precisely which aspects of household structure or characteristics of individuals most substantially influence risk of poverty. We looked first at the position of female-headed households, that is, households where the person responsible for the accommodation was a single, widowed, divorced or separated woman rather than a man or a couple. We found that in 1994, household composition and the economic status of household members were critical determinants of poverty risk. Indeed, when these factors are fully taken into account, female-headed households would otherwise have had a slightly lower risk of poverty than households headed by a single, widowed, divorced or separated man.

Changes in these characteristics accounted for some of the sharp increase in the risk of poverty for female-headed households between 1987 and 1994. The important contributory factors were the reduction in the number of adults, particularly those working for pay, in these households, and the increase in the proportion of female heads who were younger, never married or separated and with children under age 18, rather than older, widowed with no dependent children. However, these changes in the profile of female-headed households still only accounted for about one third of the increase in risk experienced by this group between 1987 and 1994.

The trends over the period in the level of social welfare support provided to different types of household are a central factor in explaining that part of the increase in risk not attributable to the profile of the households themselves. As spelt out in detail elsewhere, the policy with regard to social welfare rates followed over the 1987–1994 period was to give substantially greater increases to the schemes which, at the start of the period, provided the lowest level of support. This was consistent with the recommendations of the Commission on Social Welfare (1986) that priority be given to bringing up these lowest rates. This meant that the rates of support payable for the schemes on which many female-headed households relied lagged behind average incomes, and by 1994 were at or about the 50 per cent relative poverty line, whereas in 1987 they had been above that level. This brings out the importance of the relationship between social welfare support levels and average incomes in explaining poverty trends over time, and of the rates paid for certain schemes in particular in influencing poverty risks for female-headed households. It is worth noting in this context that since 1994 old age pensions have risen faster than unemployment payments, and that an explicit commitment has been given that the Contributory Old Age Pension rate will reach £100 per week by the year 2002.

As far as households headed by a couple are concerned, the results showed the main determinants of poverty risk to be the economic status of both partners and of others in the household, social class of the male partner and household composition (number of children and number of adults). Women's paid work was seen to reduce poverty by about the same amount as men's paid work. Additional children in the household increased poverty risk, while the presence of additional adults slightly reduced it, even if these adults were not working for pay.

The interpretation one places upon these findings and their implications depend crucially on the kind of causal ordering one sees applying to different factors. It also has implications for the most satisfactory classifications of households to employ in analysing poverty risk. For example, female-headed households may be poorer because they are likely to contain fewer adults and more children, and because the head is less likely to be working for pay, but these characteristics are themselves related to the fact that the head is a woman. Comparing female-headed households with all other households is not comparing like with like, most obviously since households headed by a couple have at least two adults, whereas many female-headed households comprise single women living alone or a woman living with dependent children. The comparison thus runs the risk of confounding household composition effects with the effects of disadvantage experienced by women. Focusing on female-headed versus all other households also runs the risk of losing sight of women living in couples, and overlooking the important contribution their paid work makes to keeping couple households out of poverty.

We then turned to a closer examination of the way in which the poverty risk of two groups, namely young unattached individuals and young lone mothers, were affected by their economic status and living arrangements. These two groups are particularly relevant here because it is the gender gap among those living alone and among lone parents that is driving the increased risk of poverty we observed for female-headed households between 1987 and 1994. The results showed that living in a larger household — for example continuing to live in the family home rather than setting up a separate household — can insulate young unattached adults and young lone mothers from the poverty risk associated with not earning an income. However, by 1994, where a lone mother works for pay living in a larger household did not further reduce poverty risk. These results clearly pointed to the "insulating" effect of sharing accommodation where the individual or lone parent is not earning. Before policy implications are drawn, however, we need to know more about the potential disadvantages of having a larger number of people sharing accommodation.

The Risk of Poverty for Women versus Men

We then shifted focus for a time from the household to the individual as the unit of analysis. This involved looking at the poverty risk for individual women and men rather than households headed by females versus males or couples, while retaining at that stage the assumption that each member of a given household has the same living standard. An overview of the risks of poverty faced by adult men and women in 1987 and 1994 showed that the gender gap in poverty risk at the individual level is much smaller than the gap between male-headed, female-headed and couple households. This is because the majority of adult men and women live in couple households, and so face similar risks of being in a poor household. It also showed that there was some increase in the poverty risk faced by adult women compared to that faced by adult men between 1987 and 1994, this being most apparent at the 60 per cent poverty line. About one third of all women, compared with 28 per cent of all men, were in households below that line in 1994.

Categorising Households in Analysing Poverty

We then went on to consider how the categorisation of households for the purpose of poverty analysis might go beyond the position of the "household head" or reference person to incorporate more of the factors which were identified as relevant to poverty risk of households. One classification system was illustrated, which allowed us to assess the positive impact of having at least one earner in the household, the importance of the presence of differing numbers of children for couple households, and the importance of women's earnings in couple households. A wide range of alternatives could be adopted, with the choice depending on the precise objective of the analysis in question. However, it is clearly both valuable and possible to employ categorisations of for example labour force status which are not based on the situation of only one individual in the household but remain analytically tractable.

Women's Employment, Low Pay and Poverty

The extent and nature of women's participation in the paid labour force is of crucial importance for women and poverty. Our analysis of women and low pay and its implications for poverty began by documenting how the increase in the overall participation rate for Irish women has outstripped that in most OECD countries since the mid-1980s, though from a low base. The ESRI samples for 1987 and 1994 showed that the percentage of married women working as employees rose from 22 per cent to 34 per cent over that period. This increase was particularly pronounced for women married to men on below-average earnings, but for women married to unemployed men the percentage in employment actually fell.

As in most other industrialised countries, women are much more likely than men to be working for low levels of pay, and the 1994 ESRI survey was then used to analyse the extent to which the earnings of female employees fell below commonly used low pay benchmarks. This showed that women comprised 41 per cent of all employees but 54 per cent of those earning below two-thirds of median hourly earnings. For those aged under 25, there was little difference between men and women in the proportion low-paid. It is women aged 25 or over, and particularly those aged 35 or over, who face a much higher risk of being in low pay than men of the same age. For example, 25 per cent of women employees between the ages of 35 and 44 earned less than two-thirds of the median, compared with only seven per cent of men in that age range. Women working part-time were also particularly likely to be low paid.

We then looked at how many of the women who are low paid were living in poor households, and the contribution which low-paid women's earnings make to keeping households out of poverty. The results showed first that the overall degree of overlap between low pay and poverty, for men or women, was quite limited. At most only about 16 per cent of low-paid individuals were members of households below the highest, 60 per cent relative income poverty line. Focusing on this minority of the low paid, a higher proportion of low-paid men than women were seen to be in poor households.

However, low pay in general and low pay for women in particular still affects a substantial proportion of that minority of poor households which do contain an employee, and is therefore highly relevant to the position of the "working poor". About 55 per cent of the employees who are in poor households have earnings below two-thirds of the median. Female employees living in poor households are generally even more likely to be low paid: two-thirds of the female employees in households below the 60 per cent relative income line are themselves earning less than two-thirds of the median. Low-paid women who are living in poor households are particularly likely to be working part-time. Again for both low-paid men and women, we also saw that a substantial proportion were in non-poor households which would be below the poverty lines if those low earnings were not coming into the household.

Women's participation in the employed labour force has widespread effects on themselves and their families beyond the income earned. One aspect of this broader context that we were able to examine here was the impact of unemployment versus employment on psychological distress levels for men versus women. The measure of psychological distress we used was the General Health Questionnaire or GHQ, which was included in the 1987 and 1994 ESRI surveys. The results presented here for 1994, like Whelan, Hannan and Creighton (1991) findings for 1987, showed that among employees women had higher GHQ scores — and thus higher levels of "stress" — than men. Among the unemployed, on the other hand, the opposite was true: women had lower stress levels on average than men. Among employees, both married men and married women had lower GHQ scores than their unmarried counterparts. For the unemployed, on the other hand, marriage is associated with higher levels of distress for men but with lower levels for women. Further, GHQ scores for married persons are in general lower when their partner is at work rather than unemployed, but for unemployed women stress levels are actually lower when their husband is unemployed than when he is at work.

Obstacles to Women's Employment

In the context of women's position in the labour force we also looked at some of the obstacles facing women who want to take up paid employment. These relate particularly to the wages paid by the jobs on offer, childcare, training and education, and disincentives built into the tax and social welfare systems. The introduction of a national hourly minimum wage along the lines recommended by the Minimum Wage Commission would clearly be a radical change in the labour market in this respect. Women make up the majority of the potential beneficiaries from a minimum wage along the lines recommended by the National Minimum Wage Commission, but it is also their jobs that would be most at risk from a minimum wage set at too high a level.

The availability and cost of childcare currently act as a major barrier to participation by women in the paid labour force. However, in addition to facilitating employment outside the home and the financial independence of women, policy in this complex area must also focus on the alleviation of poverty among children, sharing across the community of some of the costs of raising children, and the position of women in the home. Among the range of alternative policy options, child tax allowances in the income tax system or tax allowances for paid childcare would be regressive and have little impact on poor families. Alternative strategies, including direct provision of quality childcare (with priority given to disadvantaged communities) and universal support for children through child benefit, are preferable from an anti-poverty perspective.

Women seeking to re-enter the labour force after a period working full-time in the home also face barriers with respect to training. Recent research has shown that it is programmes linked closely to the labour market which are most effective in promoting participants' job prospects: general training or direct employment schemes are of themselves unlikely to do so. The crucial issue for women seeking to re-enter the labour market is thus not simply participation in programmes but progression to more advanced schemes with better linkages with the open labour market (O'Connell, 1998).

Aspects of both the tax and social welfare systems also act as barriers to women taking up paid employment. Full transferability of personal allowances and tax bands from a non-working to a working spouse means that the former faces a high tax rate on prospective earnings. A variety of disincentives to taking up paid employment can face married women or lone parents relying on social welfare transfers, particularly means-tested social assistance payments. There have been some significant improvements in this respect in recent years, notably tapered withdrawal of additional payments for "adult dependants" as the earnings of the dependent spouse increase, the recent move to assessing Family Income Supplement on a net basis, and restructuring of the means test for lone parents. However, particular problems still arise in terms of the treatment of childcare costs in assessing means, and pound for pound withdrawal of Rent Allowance as earnings rise. The broader disincentive problems created by the tax and social welfare system in combination could be tackled by targeting tax reductions on the low paid, reducing the role of means testing in the social welfare system, and providing more of the state's support for children through universal Child Benefit. Such a strategy could help to substantially ease the barriers to participation in the paid labour force currently facing women.

The Intra-household Distribution of Resources and Women's Poverty

The study then focused on the distribution of resources and living standards within the household, and the implications of any disparities in living standards between household members for poverty. Conventional methods of analysis of poverty and income inequality take the household or the narrower family as the income recipient unit, and assume resources are shared so that each individual in a given household/family has the same standard of living. Women's poverty within households with incomes above the poverty line could then be hidden, as could the extent to which women within poor households disproportionately suffer the consequences in terms of reduced consumption. In this study we sought to explore the extent of such differences within the household, employing data on non-monetary indicators of deprivation to directly measure deprivation at the level of the individual. As well as analysing differences between spouses (drawing on Cantillon and Nolan, 1998), this allowed us to look at the role which household, narrower family and individual incomes play in influencing individual deprivation levels.

We employed a set of ten non-monetary indicators which to a greater or lesser extent appeared to relate to the circumstances of the individual. For a sample of 1,763 couples, differences between spouses in responses on individual items were examined, and divergences in their scores on summary deprivation indices constructed using these items were analysed. The results showed that husband and wife gave different answers on whether they had a specific item in between five per cent and 15 per cent of couples. In about 55 per cent of the cases where differences did occur, the wife lacked the item and the husband possessed it. Constructing summary indices of deprivation using these ten items, a divergence in scores between husband and wife was seen in about half the sample couples: in about 56 per cent of these the wife had the higher deprivation score, while in 44 per cent the husband had the higher score. This general pattern was also found when subjective assessments of respondents as to whether they were doing without items because they could not afford them were used, and when only enforced lack of an item possessed by one's spouse was counted as deprivation. No systematic relationship was found between the difference in the wife's and the husband's scores on these summary deprivation indices and either household income, social class, or age. Where the wife had an income of her own the predicted gap was slightly lower, but this explained little of the actual variation we found across couples.

We then used the same set of non-monetary indicators for all individuals in the sample (not just spouses) to analyse the determinants of deprivation at individual level. In particular, we were interested to see whether it was the income accruing to the individual, the total accruing to his or her nuclear family, or the total accruing to the wider household that plays the more important role in influencing the individual's living standards. The results tend to support the argument that, given the choice between the family and the household, using the latter as income recipient unit is likely to more accurately reflect the living standards of household members. Family income does not appear as a significant influence on individual deprivation scores, whereas household income appears as a very important influence. As in previous analyses at household level, however (notably Nolan and Whelan, 1996), current household income is seen to be only one of a wide range of variables which affect deprivation, with long-term factors reflecting the accumulation or erosion of resources clearly also playing an important part.

The deprivation indicators available to us were ones employed in previous poverty studies based on large-scale survey data, designed primarily to reflect the situation of the household. The quite limited imbalance in favour of husbands shown by these indicators does not suggest that conventional poverty measurement practice "misses" substantial numbers of poor women in non-poor households, nor that policies directing resources towards poor households miss substantial numbers of women who are living outside those households but experiencing a similar level of deprivation. However, these measures were not designed with the analysis of intra-household differences in mind, and the next stage in exploring these issues will have to be the development of more sensitive indicators of deprivation designed to measure individual living standards and poverty status. Availability of information for a large sample on such specifically designed individual-level non-monetary "outcomes" measures, together with individual incomes and the way the household allocates resources, would be particularly valuable.

Key Issues and Priorities

This study has focused on areas of central importance for understanding and tackling poverty as it affects Irish women: the risk of poverty for households headed by women, women in employment and low pay, and differences in living standards within the household. It has not attempted to deal with the host of other areas and topics which would clearly be of relevance to women and poverty. It is worth reiterating in conclusion the priorities for policy highlighted by our results, bringing out their relationship with issues we have not addressed directly here, and also drawing out implications for how one frames the underlying concept of poverty itself.

The results of the study, across the range of topics dealt with, highlight the importance of both women's participation in the paid labour labour force and their treatment by the social welfare system as determinants of poverty. This focused attention first on policies aimed at reducing the various barriers to women taking up paid employment which were discussed. Second, it highlights the role of low pay and the importance of policies aimed at tackling it, including a national minimum wage and associated reconfiguration of the tax and social welfare systems. Finally, the results demonstrate the importance of ensuring that the levels of support provided by the social welfare system to those relying on it — and in this context particularly the elderly, those who have been widowed, separated or divorced, and lone parents — do not lag behind.

We have not sought to directly address a number of specific policy issues relating to, for example, the social welfare system which have clear links to these priorities. Perhaps the most important one is the issue of individualisation of social welfare payments. As the recent Social Inclusion Strategy document from the Department of Social Community and Family Affairs (1998) makes clear, this is a complex issue, and requires in-depth research in its own right. However, as that document acknowledges, the entire thrust of social welfare policy at EU level is towards the provision of individual payments (p. 120). An examination of the implications of moving in that direction for women and poverty would be able to build on the results of this study.

The final point to be made relates to the underlying concept of poverty itself. The concept of poverty adopted here and very widely is of generalised deprivation, exclusion from ordinary living conditions, due to lack of resources (see, for example, Ringen, 1987; Nolan and Whelan, 1996). This has been contrasted by some with an emphasis on poverty as a violation of the right to a minimum level of resources (Atkinson, 1987), and the relationship between these is discussed in, for example, Nolan and Whelan (1996). However, as Jenkins (1991) brings out, the poverty concept underlying the femininst critique of conventional practice appears to be rather different, relating instead to what he describes as an "individual right to a minimum degree of potential economic independence" (p. 464). As we have stressed, a situation where women do not experience much greater deprivation than men would still be entirely consistent with pervasive sex inequalities and with the concentration among husbands of the power to make major financial decisions, with consequences for power relationships within the family and economic implications for women in the event of marital breakdown. Bringing out the reality of such inequalities is important in itself, and could serve as the basis for reconceptualising poverty to include those without direct control over resources, independent of their material living standards at a given point in time. An alternative — which we would see as preferable from a conceptual and analytical perspective — is to motivate that concern in a framework which focuses on equity between men and women in the division of roles, responsibilities and power rather than on poverty *per se*.

APPENDIX 1

TABLE A3.1: LOGIT MODELS PREDICTING THE LOG-ODDS OF BEING POOR (50% POVERTY LINE) FOR NON-COUPLE HOUSEHOLDS IN 1994 (N=1122)

Mean	Variable	Model 1 Coefficient	Prob.	Model 2 Coefficient	Prob.	Model 3 Coefficient	Prob.	Model 4 Coefficient	Prob.	Model 5 Coefficient	Prob.
	Constant	-1.2702	0.0000	0.1347	0.6685	0.1137	0.7191	1.6844	0.0023	1.3818	0.0167
0.609	Head is female			0.4018	0.0174	0.3033	0.0852	0.2132	0.2366	0.2768	0.1341
57.030	Age of head			-0.0081	0.0617	-0.0075	0.1028	-0.0335	0.0000	-0.0272	0.0017
0.373	Number of children			0.4623	0.0000	0.3201	0.0017	0.1329	0.2131	0.1596	0.1471
1.474	Number of adults			-1.0707	0.0000	-1.0554	0.0000	-0.6072	0.0022	-0.5760	0.0039
0.293	Lone parent					0.4904	0.0966	-0.0035	0.9934	0.1198	0.7801
0.135	Other household type					-0.8067	0.1076	-1.2823	0.0098	-1.4108	0.0049
0.193	Pre-family household							-1.8123	0.0000	-1.7267	0.0000
0.142	Youngest child over 18							-0.8812	0.0727	-0.8598	0.0828
0.120	Head is separated/ divorced									-0.3456	0.2083
0.382	Head is widowed									-0.3807	0.0816
0.052	Head unemployed										

TABLE A3.1 Continued

Mean	Variable	Model 1 Coefficient	Model 1 Prob.	Model 2 Coefficient	Model 2 Prob.	Model 3 Coefficient	Model 3 Prob.	Model 4 Coefficient	Model 4 Prob.	Model 5 Coefficient	Model 5 Prob.
0.316	Head at work										
0.230	Head retired										
0.140	Head class 3										
0.117	Head class 4										
0.211	Head class 5										
0.187	Head class 6										
0.172	Head class 7										
0.203	Number others at work										
0.111	Number others unemployed										
0.516	Head manual social class										
0.572	Living alone										
	Log Likelihood	−590.9		−523.4		−518.5		−499.9		−498.1	
	Degrees of Freedom	0		4		6		8		10	

TABLE A3.1 Continued

Mean	Variable	Model 6 Coefficient	Prob.	Model 7 Coefficient	Prob.	Model 8 Coefficient	Prob.	Model 9 Coefficient	Prob.	Effect on average poverty rate of . . .	
	Constant	3.6832	0.0000	2.8723	0.0004	2.4649	0.0040	2.6659	0.0000		
0.609	Head is female	−0.6766	0.0116	−0.5827	0.0403	−0.5754	0.0431	−0.5133	0.0456	Female Head	−7.5%
57.030	Age of head	−0.0336	0.0012	−0.0294	0.0057	−0.0288	0.0071	−0.0376	0.0000	Head 10 years older	−5.8%
0.373	Number of children	0.1669	0.1797	0.1539	0.2205	0.1665	0.1858	0.1749	0.1089	One additional child	3.1%
1.474	Number of adults	−0.6395	0.0036	−0.6643	0.0029	−0.3155	0.3057	−0.6074	0.0064	One additional adult	−8.7%
0.293	Lone parent	−0.3773	0.4554	−0.3484	0.4960	−0.3306	0.5215				
0.135	Other household type	−1.2476	0.0226	−1.2200	0.0258	−1.3901	0.0179				
0.193	Pre-family household	−1.7850	0.0001	−1.7441	0.0001	−1.7248	0.0002	−1.9179	0.0000	Pre-family stage	−18.0%
0.142	Youngest child over 18	−0.6556	0.2260	−0.7077	0.1924	−0.5309	0.3585				
0.120	Head is separated/divorced	−0.4159	0.1840	−0.4720	0.1381	−0.4008	0.2144				
0.382	Head is widowed	−0.6307	0.0092	−0.5905	0.0157	−0.5967	0.0149	−0.4917	0.0308	Head is widowed	−7.3%
0.052	Head unemployed	0.2419	0.5244	0.2365	0.5482	0.2227	0.5728				

TABLE A3.1 Continued

Mean	Variable	Model 6		Model 7		Model 8		Model 9		Effect on average poverty rate of . . .
		Coefficient	Prob.	Coefficient	Prob.	Coefficient	Prob.	Coefficient	Prob.	
0.316	Head at work	-3.2942	0.0000	-3.1901	0.0000	-3.1804	0.0000	-3.2512	0.0000	Head at work -20.8%
0.230	Head retired	-1.9284	0.0000	-1.9750	0.0000	-1.9866	0.0000	-2.0051	0.0000	Head retired -18.3%
0.140	Head class 3			0.1799	0.6836	0.2205	0.6188			
0.117	Head class 4			0.9024	0.0296	0.9164	0.0276			
0.211	Head class 5			0.9334	0.0130	0.9116	0.0157			
0.187	Head class 6			0.5638	0.1542	0.5955	0.1339			
0.172	Head class 7			0.2280	0.5618	0.2342	0.5522			
0.203	Number others at work					-0.9765	0.0323	-0.9153	0.0294	One other at work -11.8%
0.111	Number others unemployed					-0.3933	0.3178			
0.516	Head manual social class							0.6067	0.0019	Manual social class 12.1%
0.572	Living Alone							0.8024	0.0301	Living alone 16.6%
	Log Likelihood	-404.4		-397.8		-395.2		-398.2		
	Degrees of Freedom	13		21		27		11		

TABLE A3.4: SET OF LOGIT MODELS PREDICTING THE LOG-ODDS OF BEING POOR (50% POVERTY LINE) FOR COUPLE HOUSEHOLDS IN 1994 (N=2922)

Mean	Model	1 Coefficient	1 Prob.	2 Coefficient	2 Prob.	3 Coefficient	3 Prob.	4 Coefficient	4 Prob.	5 Coefficient	5 Prob.	6 Coefficient	6 Prob.
1.000		-1.5973	0.0000	-2.0647	0.0000	-0.2273	0.6650	0.0437	0.9433	1.8306	0.0086	0.6666	0.3684
48.005	Age of male partner			0.0068	0.1539	-0.0185	0.0199	0.0035	0.7209	0.0243	0.1175	0.0260	0.0931
1.549	Number children (under 18)			0.4794	0.0000	0.5266	0.0000	0.4725	0.0000	0.4506	0.0000	0.4546	0.0000
2.593	Number adults (18+)			-0.3044	0.0000	-0.2126	0.0064	-0.4932	0.0000	-0.4953	0.0000	-0.5220	0.0000
0.066	Pre-family					-1.7057	0.0001	-0.3538	0.4579	-0.0561	0.9149	0.0159	0.9758
0.270	Youngest child <5					-1.3307	0.0001	-0.3501	0.3610	-0.8095	0.0617	-0.7217	0.0990
0.152	Youngest 5-9					-1.2364	0.0001	-0.3805	0.2945	-0.7238	0.0697	-0.6899	0.0870
0.211	Youngest 10-17					-0.7544	0.0058	0.3043	0.3249	0.0998	0.7678	0.1336	0.6952
0.151	Youngest 18+					-1.1014	0.0005	-0.5993	0.0669	-0.8429	0.0147	-0.8262	0.0177
0.124	Male partner unemployed							0.7228	0.0023	0.5272	0.0388	0.4942	0.0544
0.677	Male Partner at work							-2.2060	0.0000	-2.3528	0.0000	-2.1738	0.0000
0.154	Male partner retired							-1.1877	0.0001	-1.3853	0.0000	-1.3747	0.0000
0.009	Female partner unemployed									-11.4768	0.9332	-11.4851	0.9334
0.295	Female partner at work									-2.1152	0.0000	-2.1054	0.0000
0.015	Female Partner retired									-2.1696	0.0748	-2.1532	0.0775

TABLE A3.4: Continued

Age of female partner	45.408				-0.0428	0.0132	-0.0398	0.0217
Male partner SC 2	0.117						0.6647	0.0342
Male partner SC 3	0.162						0.6772	0.0160
Male partner SC 4	0.270						1.1313	0.0000
Male partner SC 5	0.124						1.0476	0.0002
Male partner SC 6	0.105						0.9837	0.0006
Male partner SC 7	0.058						1.0691	0.0009
Female partner SC 2	0.143							
Female partner SC 3	0.269							
Female partner SC 4	0.039							
Female partner SC 5	0.286							
Female partner SC 6	0.106							
Female partner SC 7	0.121							
N. others at work	0.315							
N. others unemployed	0.100							
Female partner over 65	0.106							
Log Likelihood	-1324.4	-1195.3	-1180.8	-951.8	-872.6		-859.0	
Degrees of Freedom	0	3	8	11	15		21	

TABLE A3.4: Continued

Mean	Model	7 Coefficient	7 Prob.	8 Coefficient	8 Prob.	9 Coefficient	9 Prob.	Effect on average poverty rate of . . .	
1.000		1.0755	0.1963	-0.4090	0.6379	-0.0482	0.8982		
48.005	Age of male partner	0.0250	0.1116	0.0270	0.0908				
1.549	Number children (under 18)	0.4624	0.0000	0.4798	0.0000	0.4028	0.0000	One additional child	6.4%
2.593	Number adults (18+)	-0.5346	0.0000	0.1366	0.3102	-0.1928	0.0554	One additional adult	-2.5%
0.066	Pre-family	-0.0299	0.9547	0.0406	0.9395				
0.270	Youngest child <5	-0.7814	0.0748	-0.8061	0.0708	-0.3739	0.0149	Youngest child under 4	-4.6%
0.152	Youngest 5–9	-0.6976	0.0843	-0.7080	0.0845				
0.211	Youngest 10–17	0.0869	0.7993	0.2182	0.5300				
0.151	Youngest 18+	-0.8707	0.0128	-0.8301	0.0227	-0.8474	0.0059	Youngest child over 18	-8.9%
0.124	Male partner unemployed	0.4393	0.0883	0.5328	0.0447				
0.677	Male Partner at work	-2.1404	0.0000	-2.1730	0.0000	-2.4586	0.0000	Husb. at work	-15.1%
0.154	Male partner retired	-1.3957	0.0000	-1.4110	0.0000	-1.1130	0.0000	Husb. retired	-10.6%
0.009	Female partner unemployed	-11.4615	0.9333	-11.7311	0.9303				
0.295	Female partner at work	-2.1157	0.0000	-2.1534	0.0000	-2.1383	0.0000	Wife at work	-14.5%
0.015	Female Partner retired	-2.1680	0.0765	-2.0982	0.0867				
45.408	Age of female partner	-0.0403	0.0215	-0.0416	0.0199				

TABLE A3.4: Continued

0.117	Male partner SC 2	0.6518	0.0394	0.6292	0.0494	0.6593	0.0366	Husb. class 2	11.3%
0.162	Male partner SC 3	0.6408	0.0246	0.7077	0.0133	0.7021	0.0123	Husb. class 3	12.2%
0.270	Male partner SC 4	1.0586	0.0000	1.0815	0.0000	1.0804	0.0000	Husb. class 4	20.5%
0.124	Male partner SC 5	0.8943	0.0018	0.9265	0.0014	0.9437	0.0008	Husb. class 5	17.4%
0.105	Male partner SC 6	0.8582	0.0034	0.8572	0.0039	0.7913	0.0060	Husb. class 6	14.0%
0.058	Male partner SC 7	0.9648	0.0034	1.0332	0.0021	1.0517	0.0012	Husb. class 7	19.9%
0.143	Female partner SC 2	-0.2203	0.6258	-0.2255	0.6204				
0.269	Female partner SC 3	-0.6900	0.1035	-0.6406	0.1324	-0.6769	0.0000	Wife class 3	-7.5%
0.039	Female partner SC 4	-0.2230	0.6476	-0.0298	0.9516				
0.286	Female partner SC 5	-0.0408	0.9213	-0.0205	0.9605				
0.106	Female partner SC 6	-0.0907	0.8359	-0.0650	0.8828				
0.121	Female partner SC 7	-0.0700	0.8709	0.0723	0.8674				
0.315	N. others at work			-1.8263	0.0000	-1.3537	0.0000	One other at work	-11.9%
0.100	N. others unemployed			-0.5371	0.0031				
0.106	Female partner over 65					-1.6596	0.0000	Wife over age 65	-13.1%
	Log Likelihood	-851.5		-817.9		-832.0			
	Degrees of Freedom	27		29		28			

REFERENCES

Abowitz, D.A. (1986), "Data Indicate the Feminization of Poverty in Canada, Too", *Sociology and Social Research*, Vol. 70, No. 3, April, pp. 209–213.

Arber, S. and J. Ginn (1991), *Gender and Later Life: a Sociological Analysis of Resources and Constraints*, CI, Newbury Park, CA: Sage Publications, Inc.

Arditti, J.A. (1997), "Women, Divorce, and Economic Risk", *Family and Conciliation Courts Review*, Vol. 35, No. 1, January pp. 79–89.

Atkinson, A.B. (1987), "On the Measurement of Poverty", *Econometrica*, Vol. 55, No. 4, 749–764.

Baron, J.N. and A.E. Newman (1990), "For What It's Worth: Organizations, Occupations, and the Value of Work Done by Women and Nonwhites", *American Sociological Review*, Vol. 55, No. 2, April, pp. 155–175.

Barrett, A., T. Callan and B. Nolan (1998), "Rising Wage Inequality, Returns to Education and Labour Market Institutions: Evidence from Ireland", *British Journal of Industrial Relations*, forthcoming.

Bazen, S. (1988), *On the Overlap Between Low Pay and Poverty*, Discussion Paper 120, Programme on Taxation, Incentives and the Distribution of Income, London: London School of Economics.

Bernhardt, A., M. Morris and M.S. Handcock, (1995), "Women's Gains or Men's Losses? A Closer Look at the Shrinking Gender Gap in Earnings", *American Journal of Sociology*, Vol. 101, No. 2, September, pp. 302–328.

Blackburn, R.J. (1995), "Comparable Worth and the Fair Pay Act of 1994", *Kentucky Law Journal*, Vol. 84, No. 4, pp. 1277–1302.

Blackwell, J. (1986), *Low Pay: The Current Position and Policy Issues*, Resource and Environmental Policy Centre, University College Dublin, mimeo.

Blackwell, J. (1987), *Low Pay and Women*, Working Paper 45, Resource and Environmental Policy Centre, University College Dublin, mimeo.

Blackwell, J. (1989), *Low Pay in Ireland*, Resource and Environmental Policy Centre, University College Dublin, mimeo.

Blau, F.D. (1993), "Gender and Economic Outcomes: The Role of Wage Structure", *Labour*, Vol. 7, No. 1, Spring, pp. 73–92.

Bose, C.E. (1989), "Ethnicity, Gender and Poverty: A Comparative Analysis of Cubans, Mexicans and Puerto Ricans", paper presented at the Annual Meeting of the American Sociological Association.

Boston, T.D. (1990), "Segmented Labor Markets: New Evidence from a Study of Four Race Gender Groups", *Industrial and Labor Relations Review*, Vol. 44, No. 1, October, pp. 99–115.

Breen, R. and C.T. Whelan (1996), *Social Mobility and Social Class in Ireland*, Dublin: Gill and Macmillan.

Brereton, D. (1990), "Gender Differences in Overtime", *Journal of Industrial Relations*, Vol. 32, No. 3, September, pp. 370–385.

Burkhauser, R. and T. Finnegan (1989), "The Minimum Wage and the Poor: The End of a Relationship?", *Journal of Policy Analysis and Management*, Vol. 8, No. 1, pp. 53–71.

Callan, T. (1994), "Poverty and Gender Inequality", in B. Nolan and T. Callan, (eds), *Poverty and Policy in Ireland*, Dublin: Gill and Macmillan.

Callan, T. and B. Farrell (1991), *Women's Participation in the Irish Labour Market*, Report No. 91, Dublin: National Economic and Social Council.

Callan, T., B. Nolan and C.T. Whelan (1993), "Resources, Deprivation and the Measurement of Poverty", *Journal of Social Policy*, Vol. 22, No. 2, pp. 141–172.

Callan, T., B. Nolan and B.J. Whelan, D.F. Hannan with S. Creighton (1989), *Poverty, Income and Welfare in Ireland*, General Research Series No. 146, Dublin: The Economic and Social Research Institute.

Callan, T., B. Nolan, and C.T. Whelan, (1996), *A Review of the Commission on Social Welfare's Minimum Adequate Income*, Policy Research Series No. 29, Dublin: The Economic and Social Research Institute.

Callan, T., C. O'Donoghue and C. O'Neill (1994), *Analysis of Basic Income Schemes for Ireland*, Dublin: Economic and Social Research Institute.

Callan, T., B. Nolan, D. O'Neill and O. Sweetman (1999), *The Distribution of Income in Ireland*, Dublin: Oak Tree Press/Combat Poverty Agency, forthcoming.

Callan, T., B. Nolan, B.J. Whelan, C.T. Whelan, and J. Williams, (1996), *Poverty in the 1990s: Evidence from the Living in Ireland Survey*, General Research Series Paper 170, Dublin: Oak Tree Press/Combat Poverty Agency.

Callan, T. and A. Wren (1994), *Male–Female Wage Differentials: Analysis and Policy Issues*, General Research Series, Dublin: The Economic and Social Research Institute.

Cantillon, S. (1994), *Inequality Within the Home: Women and Poverty*, unpublished thesis for Master of Equality Studies, Dublin: UCD.

Cantillon, S. (1997), "Women and Poverty: Differences in Living Standards Within Households", in A. Byrne and M. Leonard (eds), *Women and Irish Society: A Sociological Reader*, Belfast: Beyond the Pale Publications.

Cantillon, S. and B. Nolan (1998), "Are Married Women More Deprived than their Husbands?", *Journal of Social Policy*, Vol. 27, No. 2, pp. 151–171.

Carney, C., E. FitzGerald, G. Kiely, and P. Quinn, (1994), *The Cost of a Child*, Dublin: Combat Poverty Agency.

Central Statistics Office (1996), *Labour Force Survey 1995*, Dublin: Stationery Office.

Central Statistics Office (1997), *Household Budget Survey 1994-95 Volume 1: Detailed Results for All Households*, Dublin: Stationery Office.

Centre d'Études des Revenus et des Coutes (1991), *Les Bas Salaires dans les Pays de la Communauté Économique Européenne*, Paris: CERC.

Clark, C. and J. Healy (1997), *Pathways to a Basic Income*, Dublin: Conference of Religious of Ireland.

Commission on Social Welfare (1986), *Report of the Commission on Social Welfare*, Dublin: Stationery Office.

Commission on the Family (1998), "Strengthening Families for Life", Final Report to the Minister for Social, Community and Family Affairs, Dublin: Stationery Office.

Commission on the Status of Women (1993), "Report to Government", Dublin: Stationery Office.

Conniffe, D. and G. Keogh (1988), *Equivalence Scales and Costs of Children*, General Research Series Paper No. 142, Dublin: The Economic and Social Research Institute.

Conroy, P. (1993), "Managing the Mothers: the Case of Ireland", in J. Lewis (ed.), *Women and Social Policies in Europe, Work, Family and the State*, Aldershot: Edward Elgar.

Conroy, P. (1997), "Lone Mothers: The Case of Ireland", in J. Lewis (ed.) *Lone Mothers in Europe*, Jessica Langley.

Daly, M. (1989), *Women and Poverty*, Dublin: Attic Press.

Davies, H. and H. Joshi (1994), "Sex, Sharing and the Distribution of Income", *Journal of Social Policy*, Vol. 23, No. 3, pp. 301–340.

Davies, H. and H. Joshi (1998), "Gender and Income Inequality in the UK, 1968–1990: The Feminization of Earnings or of Poverty?", *Statistics in Society: Journal of the Royal Statistical Society*, Vol. 161, Part 1, pp.33–61.

Department of Social, Community and Family Affairs (1998), *Social Inclusion Strategy*, Dublin: Stationery Office.

Doucet, A. (1995), "Gender Equality and Gender Differences in Household Work and Parenting", *Women's Studies International Forum*, Vol. 18, No. 3, May–June, pp. 271–284.

Duffy, C. (1994), "Female Poverty, Powerlessness and Social Exclusion in Ireland", *Administration*, Vol. 42, No. 1, pp. 47–66.

Duncan, K.C. (1996), "Gender Differences in the Effect of Education on the Slope of Experience Earnings Profiles: National Longitudinal Survey of Youth, 1979–1988", *American Journal of Economics and Sociology*, Vol. 55, No. 4, October, pp. 457–471.

Durkan, J. with A. O'Donohue, M. Donnelly, and J. Durkan (1995), *Women in the Labour Force*, Dublin: Employment Equality Agency.

Erikson, R. (1984), "Social Class of Men, Women and Families", *Sociology*, Vol. 18, No. 4, pp. 500–514.

Ermisch, J., S.P. Jenkins and R.E. Wright (1989), "Adverse Selection Aspects of Poverty Amongst Lone Mothers", *Birkbeck College Discussion Papers in Economics*, Vol. 89, No. 2, January, pp. 28.

Fahey, T. and M. Lyons (1995), *Marital Breakdown and Family Law in Ireland: a Sociological Study*, Dublin: The Economic and Social Research Institute/Oak Tree Press.

Fahey, T. (1998), "Childcare Policy Options", in *Budget Perspectives: Proceedings of a conference held on 27 October 1998*, T. Callan (ed.), Dublin: The Economic and Social Research Institute.

Felstead, A. (1996), "Identifying Gender Inequalities in the Distribution of Vocational Qualifications in the UK", *Gender, Work and Organization*, Vol. 3, No. 1, January, pp. 38–50.

Figart, D.M. and J. Lapidus (1995), "A Gender Analysis of US Labor Market Policies for the Working Poor", *Feminist Economics*, Vol. 1, No. 3, fall, pp. 60–81.

Findlay, J. and R.E. Wright (1996), "Gender, Poverty and the Intra-household Distribution of Resources", *Review of Income and Wealth*, Vol. 42, No. 3, September, pp. 335–51.

Finnie, R. (1993), "Women, Men, and the Economic Consequences of Divorce: Evidence from Canadian Longitudinal Data", *Revue Canadienne de Sociologie et d'Anthropologie / Canadian Review of Sociology and Anthropology*, Vol. 30, No. 2, pp. 205–241.

Freyman, H., J. Mack, S. Lansley, D. Gordon and J. Hills (1991), *Breadline Britain 1990s: The Findings of the Television Series*, London: London Weekend Television.

Garfinkel, I. and S. McLanahan (1986), *Single Mothers and Their Children: A New American Dilemma*, Washington DC: Urban Institute Press.

Ginn, J. and S. Arber (1991), "Gender, Class and Income Inequalities in Later Life", *British Journal of Sociology*, Vol. 42, No. 3, September, pp. 369–396.

Goldberg, G.S., E. Kremen, (1987), "The Feminization of Poverty: Only in America?", *Social Policy*, Vol. 17, No. 4, spring, pp. 3–14.

Goldberg, G.S., E. Kremen, J. Axinn, J. Jenson, R. Kantrow, M. Rosenthal and S. Wojciechowski, (eds.) (1990), *The Feminization of Poverty: Only in America?*, New York, NY: Praeger.

Graham, H. (1987), "Women's Poverty and Caring", in C. Glendinning and J. Millar (eds.), *Women and Poverty in Britain*, Sussex: Harvester Wheatsheaf.

Graham, H. (1994), "Breadline Motherhood: Trends and Experiences in Ireland", *Administration*, Vol. 42, No. 3, pp. 352–73.

Green, E.E., and D.M. Woodward (1990), "'To Them That Hath . . .' Inequality and Social Control in Women's Leisure", Association Paper: International Sociological Association (ISA).

Hardy, M.A. L. Hazelrigg, (1993), "The Gender of Poverty in an Ageing Population", *Research on Ageing*, Vol. 15, No. 3, September, pp. 243–278.

Harkness, S., S. Machin and J. Waldfogel (1997), "Evaluating the Pin Money Hypothesis: The Relationship between Women's Labour Market Activity, Family Income and Poverty in Britain", *Journal of Population Economics*, Vol. 10, No. 2, May, pp. 137, 58.

Hatch, L.R. (1990), "Gender and Work at Midlife and Beyond", *Generations*, Vol. 14, No. 3, summer, pp. 48–52.

Hayes, L. (1990), *Working for Change: A Study of Three Women's Community Projects*, CPA Report Research Series No. 8, Dublin: Combat Poverty Agency.

Heimer, C.A. (1996), "Gender Inequalities in the Distribution of Responsibility", in J.N. Baron, D. Grusky, and D.J. Treiman (eds.), *Social Differentiation and Social Inequality: Essays in Honor of John Pock*, , Boulder, CO: Westview Press.

Howell, F.M. and D.R. Bronson (1996), "The Journey to Work and Gender Inequality in Earnings: A Cross Validation Study for the United States", *Sociological Quarterly*, Vol. 37, No. 3, Summer, pp. 429–447.

Integrating Tax and Social Welfare — Report of the Expert Working Group on the Integration of the Tax and Social Welfare Systems (1996), Dublin: Stationery Office.

Jenkins, S.P. (1991), "Poverty Measurement and the Within-household Distribution: Agenda for Action", *Journal of Social Policy*, Vol. 20, Part 4, pp. 457–83.

Johnson, P. and S. Webb (1989), "Counting People with Low Incomes: the Impact of Recent Changes in Official Statistics", *Fiscal Studies*, Vol. 10, No. 4, pp. 66–82.

Joyce, L. and A. McCashin (1982), *Poverty and Social Policy in Ireland*, Dublin: Institute of Public Administration.

Kelleghan, T. and P.J. Fontes (1988), "Gender Differences in the Scholastic Self-Concept of Irish Pupils", *Irish Journal of Education*, Vol. 22, pp. 42–52.

Kennedy, S. ed. (1981), *One Million Poor? The Challenge of Irish Inequality*, Dublin: Turoe Press.

Layard, R., D. Piachaud and M. Stewart *et al.* (1978), *The Causes of Poverty*, Background Paper No. 5, Royal Commission on the Distribution of Income and Wealth, London: HMSO.

Lynch, K. (1989), *The Hidden Curriculum: Reproduction in Education, an Appraisal*, East Sussex: Falmer Press.

Mack, J. and S. Lansley (1985), *Poor Britain*, London: Allen and Unwin.

Marini, M.M. and P.L. Fan (1997), "The Gender Gap in Earnings at Career Entry", *American Sociological Review*, Vol. 62, No. 4, August, pp. 588–604.

Marklund, S. (1990), "Structures of Modern Poverty", *Acta Sociologica*, Vol. 33, No. 2, pp. 125–140.

Mayer, S. and C. Jencks, (1988), "Poverty and the Distribution of Material Hardship", *Journal of Human Resources*, Vol. 24, No. 1, pp. 88–114.

McCashin, A. (1993), *Lone Parents in the Republic of Ireland: Enumeration, Description and Implications for Social Policy*, Dublin: The Economic and Social Research Institute.

McCashin, A. (1996), *Lone Mothers in Ireland: a Local Study*, Dublin: Combat Poverty Agency/Oak Tree Press.

McCashin, A. (1997), "Employment Aspects of Young Lone Parenthood in Ireland", Dublin: Department of Social Studies, Trinity College.

McLanahan, S., A. Sørensen, and D. Watson (1989), "Sex Differences in Poverty, 1950–1980", *Signs*, Vol. 15, No. 1, pp. 102–122.

McMahon, G. (1987), "Wage Structure in the Republic of Ireland", *Advances in Business Studies*, Vol. 1, No. 1, pp. 13–27.

Meyer, M.H. (1990), "Family Status and the Gendered Distribution of Retirement Income", Association Paper, American Sociological Association.

Millar, J. and C. Glendinning (1987), "Invisible Women, Invisible Poverty", in C. Glendinning and J. Millar (eds.), *Women and Poverty in Britain*, Sussex: Harvester Wheatsheaf.

Millar, J., C. Davies and S. Leaper (1992), *Lone Parents, Poverty and Public Policy in Ireland*, Dublin: Combat Poverty Agency.

Murphy, T., Deloitte and Touche (1998), *Review of Community Employment Programme Final Report*, Dublin: The Stationery Office.

National Minimum Wage Commission (1998a), *Report, Volume 1*, Dublin: Stationery Office.

National Minimum Wage Commission (1998b), *Report, Volume 2, Low Pay in Ireland* by B. Nolan, Dublin: Stationery Office.

Nolan, B. (1989), "An Evaluation of the New Low Income Statistics", *Fiscal Studies*, Vol. 10, No. 4, pp. 53–66.

Nolan, B. (1993), *Low Pay in Ireland*, General Research Series Paper No. 159, Dublin: The Economic and Social Research Institute.

Nolan, B. and T. Callan (eds.) (1994), *Poverty and Policy in Ireland*, Dublin: Gill and Macmillan.

Nolan, B. and C.T. Whelan (1996), *Resources, Deprivation and Poverty*, Oxford: Clarendon Press.

Norris, P. (1984), "Women in Poverty: Britain and America", *Social Policy*, Vol. 14, No. 4, Spring, pp. 41–43.

Northrop, E.M. (1990), "The Feminization of Poverty: The Demographic Factor and the Composition of Economic Growth", *Journal of Economic Issues*, Vol. 24, No. 1, pp. 145–160.

Ó Cinnéide, S. (1972), "The Extent of Poverty in Ireland", *Social Studies*, Vol. 1, No. 4, pp. 381–400.

O'Connell, P. (1998), "Spending Priorities in Labour Market Programmes for the Unemployed", in T. Callan (ed.), *Budget Perspectives: Proceedings of a Conference Held on 27 October 1998*, Dublin: The Economic and Social Research Institute.

O'Connell, P. and F. McGinnity (1997), Working Schemes? Active Labour Market Policy in Ireland, Aldershot: Ashgate.

OECD (1996), *Employment Outlook*, Paris: OECD.

O'Neill, C. (1992), *Telling It Like It Is*, Dublin: Combat Poverty Agency.

Pearce, D. (1978), "The Feminization of Poverty: Women, Work and Welfare", *Urban and Social Change Review*, Vol. 11, pp. 28–36.

Petersen, T. and L.A. Morgan (1995), "Separate and Unequal: Occupation Establishment Sex Segregation and the Gender Wage Gap", *American Journal of Sociology*, Vol. 101, No. 2, September, pp. 329–365.

Presser, H.B. and J.M. Hermsen (1996), "Gender Differences in the Determinants of Work Related Overnight Travel among Employed Americans", *Work and Occupations*, Vol. 23, No. 1, pp. 87–115.

Richardson, V. and N. Winston (1989), *Unmarried Mothers Delivered in the National Maternity Hospital 1987*, Dublin: Department of Social Work and Administration, UCD.

Ringen, S. (1987), *The Possibility of Politics*, Oxford: Clarendon Press.

Roche, J. (1984), *Poverty and Income Maintenance Policies in Ireland 1973–80*, Dublin: Institute of Public Administration.

Rosenfeld, R.A. and A.L. Kalleberg (1991), "Gender Inequality in the Labor Market: A Cross National Perspective", *Acta Sociologica*, Vol. 34, No. 3, pp. 207–225.

Ross, C.E. and J. Mirowsky (1996), "Economic and Interpersonal Work Rewards: Subjective Utilities of Men's and Women's Compensation", *Social Forces*, Vol. 75, No. 1, September, pp. 223–246.

Rottman, D. (1993), *Income Distribution within Irish Households: Allocating Resources Within Irish Families*, Dublin: Combat Poverty Agency.

Rottman, D. (1994), "Allocating Money Within Households: Better Off Poorer?", in B. Nolan and T. Callan (eds.), *Poverty and Policy in Ireland*, Dublin: Gill and Macmillan.